HIPAA
by Example

Mary C. Thomason, MSA, RHIA, CHPS, CISSP

Jill Callahan Dennis, JD, RHIA
Technical Reviewer

AHIMA
American Health Information
Management Association®

ISBN 1-58426-180-3
ISBN 978 1-58426-180-3
AHIMA Product No. AB121107

Jill Callahan Dennis, JD, RHIA, Technical Reviewer
Lou Ann Wiedemann MS, RHIA, Reviewer

Ken Zielske, Director of Publications
Kimberly L. Hines, MS, Project Editor
Melissa Ulbricht, Editorial/Production Coordinator
Katie Greenock, Assistant Editor

Any Web sites listed in this book were current and valid as of the date of publication. However, Web page addresses and the information on them may change or disappear at any time and for any number of reasons. The user is encouraged to perform general Web searches to locate any site addresses listed here that are no longer valid.

AHIMA strives to recognize the value of people from every racial and ethnic background as well as all genders, age groups, and sexual orientations by building its membership and leadership resources to reflect the rich diversity of the American population. AHIMA encourages the celebration and promotion of human diversity through education, mentoring, recognition, leadership, and other programs.

American Health Information Management Association
233 North Michigan Avenue, 21st Floor
Chicago, Illinois 60601-5800

www.ahima.org

CONTENTS

SECTION I
Administration and Organization Issues

SECTION II
Reducing Incidental Disclosures with Reasonable Safeguards

SECTION III
It's the Law

SECTION IV
Employee Records and HIPAA

SECTION V
An Individual's Rights and Permission to Disclose

SECTION VI
Treatment, Payment, and Healthcare Operations

SECTION VII
Sanctions and Compliance

SECTION VIII
Special Use and Disclosure Situations

ABOUT THE AUTHOR

Mary Thomason, MSA, RHIA, CHPS, CISSP, is currently a senior compliance consultant at Intermountain Healthcare, a large integrated health system in Salt Lake City, Utah, which employs 27,000 people. Her focus, beginning in 2001, has been to assist Intermountain in initial and ongoing compliance with the Privacy Rule. She is currently chair of the Intermountain Privacy Board. Prior to working in compliance, she was a project manager for software installation for Intermountain information systems and, at another point, director of medical records at one of the Intermountain facilities.

The author is also an active member of the Utah HIPAA Pre-emption Task Force. The governor of Utah, to complete an analysis of Utah law and HIPAA, originally chartered this group, comprising representatives from healthcare institutions throughout Utah. The task force has continued to actively meet and review new laws and to deal with other issues related to health privacy in the state of Utah. The task force met last year with federal, state, and local law enforcement officials to analyze how state law and HIPAA interact in regards to law enforcement activities.

As a member of the American Health Information Management Association (AHIMA), Mary was part of the initial construction committee to create the Certification in Healthcare Privacy (CHP). She continues now as a member of the Certification in Healthcare Privacy and Security (CHPS) construction committee. She is an active contributor to HIPAA's Community of Practice (CoP). Mary spoke at the AHIMA national convention in 2006, on the subject of HIPAA and research. She has been a frequent speaker, as well, for the Utah Health Information Management Association (UHIMA). She has also served UHIMA in many capacities, as president, treasurer, and long-time legislative committee chair.

ACKNOWLEDGMENTS

The author wishes to thank Jill Callahan Dennis, JD, RHIA, for taking time out of an already busy schedule to provide the technical review of this book.

The author also wishes to thank those who contributed to AHIMA's HIPAA CoP for articulating current issues and thoughts on implementation from the real world of healthcare privacy.

Finally, the author wishes to thank her husband for boundless encouragement and support in whatever she undertakes.

ABOUT THE TECHNICAL REVIEWER

Jill Callahan Dennis, JD, RHIA is principal of **Health Risk Advantage**, a Colorado-based risk management consulting firm for healthcare organizations. Her leadership on information privacy issues spans many years, as author of the book "Privacy and Confidentiality of Health Information," numerous articles, and her role as faculty for a nationwide series of AHIMA seminars on health information privacy issues. She is currently a member of the Confidentiality, Privacy, and Security Workgroup of the U.S. Department of Health and Human Service's American Health Information Community (AHIC).

She is a frequent speaker on HIPAA compliance and privacy matters and was the 2006 President of the Board of Directors for the American Health Information Management Association.

INTRODUCTION

The Health Insurance Portability and Accountability Act (HIPAA) Privacy Rule was heralded by most healthcare providers and health plans in the midst of a flurry of policy writing, notice printing, and training classes to be completed by the HIPAA implementation date of April of 2003. Time to move on to new challenges, right?

The reality has been otherwise. Implementation of the Privacy Rule continues to be an area of confusion and struggle, and the longer it is in effect the greater the number of problems generated. For members of the American Health Information Management Association (AHIMA), the HIPAA Communities of Practice (CoP) is one of the most active forums that AHIMA maintains, in which lively and profound discussions occur every day regarding HIPAA implementation. The scenarios contained in this book originated from the AHIMA HIPAA CoP and related AHIMA CoPs. These scenarios date not from the early days of implementation of HIPAA, but instead, from the last few years up to the end of 2006. The CoP scenarios are used to illustrate the range of issues that continue to surface regarding Privacy Rule implementation, as well as tap into the knowledge of the participants, who are by and large, deeply involved and highly expert in the continuing implementation of the Privacy Rule.

HIPAA Privacy Rule implementation is not simple. HIPAA Privacy Rule compliance is extremely complex. Why does the Privacy Rule implementation still remain such a struggle? The first reason is that the Privacy Rule was written largely with paper records in mind, as those who have attempted to implement some of its provisions, such as the right to request restrictions, can testify. (See scenario 68: "When should we honor restriction requests?") The adaptation of electronic systems used to store protected health information has introduced many new variables to Privacy Rule implementation that could not have been anticipated when the Rule was written. (See scenarios 2, 55, and 130: "Should we restrict access of physicians to our electronic record? Should employees be allowed to access their own protected health information electronically? Is it possible to allow parents access to a child's records online?")

The second reason is that the writers of the Rule based the Rule upon their understanding of basic healthcare and health plan activities. However, the healthcare environment is extremely complex, and healthcare communication does not always occur in traditional ways. For example, a standard imposed by the Privacy Rule is that a healthcare provider or health plan may only disclose the protected health information of an individual to the individual's family based on the individual's agreement. Further, they must limit the information to that which addresses the immediate need based on the involvement of the family in the treatment of the individual. The environment addressed in the Privacy Rule is a clinical setting in which the patient is present and is queried about his or her preferences on sharing information with family. In the worst case, the patient is unconscious, and the healthcare provider is left to determine the patient's prior preferences or to use professional judgment to make a decision about what can be shared. In reality, thousands, if not millions, of interactions occur every day with families calling to inquire about patients over the phone, interacting with employees who are not healthcare professionals. What is required to establish the identity of family, the preference of the individual, and the amount of information that can be shared when this occurs? Many covered entities have set such high standards in these situations to meet what they believe the Privacy Rule requires that they have alienated the individuals they are trying to serve. (See scenarios 75, 76, 77, and 79: "How do healthcare providers know when it is okay to talk to family about a patient? How can family passwords or codes be implemented to verify identity? Can parents of adults set up appointments? May another person pick up copies of records on an adult patient without an authorization?")

Finally, the decision the writers of the Privacy Rule made to not pre-empt all state laws or other laws or regulations in regards to health information makes the rule even more difficult to implement. It is vital to understand state laws and privacy in regards to personal representatives, minors, and law enforcement reporting and interactions. Most of the scenarios written in this book do not have a clear yes or no answer, largely because the answer is dependent on the interaction of other laws and regulations. The reader is invited to review the book and see how many times the following symbols appear. These symbols indicate that state and federal laws; alcohol and substance abuse laws, international laws, and worker's compensation laws may apply.

 State and federal laws

 Alcohol and substance abuse laws

 International laws

 State and federal labor and worker's compensation laws

There were pre-emption analyses performed in most states, but the analyses were usually performed only one time, in 2003, because these analyses are expensive and time-consuming. Unfortunately, state laws change all the time, so chances are good that an analysis performed in 2003 is not adequate today. Because state laws have the major impact on implementation of the Privacy Rule, links to each state's statutes are included in an appendix in this book.

HOW TO USE THIS BOOK

How should this book be used? It is not to be considered legal advice, even though it has been carefully reviewed. I am not an attorney, nor is this a reflection of the opinions of my employer. Because implementation of the Privacy Rule is so dependent on state laws, a covered entity should consult its own legal counsel before implementing the answers in this book.

However, the answers to the scenarios are based on best practices as shared in the AHIMA HIPAA CoP analysis of the Privacy Rule itself, study of the extensive commentary to the Privacy Rule, and publications and statements from the Office for Civil Rights (OCR) and professional groups, such as AHIMA. Other federal government agency publications were also reviewed, as pertinent. Each scenario is referenced for the source of the answer. Readers are strongly encouraged to become familiar with their own state laws or other laws and regulations that may apply to their covered entity and, using the scenario answers, arrive at customized answers for their own situations.

As the author, I have been involved in implementation, support, and compliance monitoring of the Privacy Rule in a large, extremely complex healthcare system that also includes a health plan. Because it is my assignment to only handle Privacy Rule compliance, I receive questions about privacy rule implementation every day. I have the responsibility to research each question thoroughly using all available references. I use my background in health information management and clinical care to determine "reasonable" answers to questions of how to implement the Privacy Rule in a given scenario. I have also had the opportunity to consult with very fine legal counsel in the course of my work and also as a member of the ongoing Utah HIPAA Pre-emption and Law Enforcement task force. I have the deepest respect for the knowledge and intellect of both my employer's legal counsel and members of the task force and appreciate their patience in explaining the complexity of how laws and regulations interact.

Finally, a word of caution: as one of my legal counsel friends explained to me, the Privacy Rule, as implemented, should be considered the "bones" of health privacy. Published documents, such as the commentary or the Frequently Asked Questions on the Privacy Rule from the OCR, or books like this, may outline the shape around the "bones." However, only case and administrative law decisions will flesh out the "bones," and ultimately define the way the Privacy Rule must be implemented.

SECTION I

Administration and Organization Issues

This section describes HIPAA Privacy Rule requirements for agreements between covered entities, or between a covered entity and other entities that are not covered under the Privacy Regulations. It also includes scenarios concerning business associates and compliance issues with external vendors.

Scenario 1

If we expand our Organized Health Care Arrangement (OHCA) to include other nonowned hospitals, may we provide information technology services for them?

An Organized Health Care Arrangement (OHCA) is not the appropriate agreement to cover this type of service. In this situation, a more applicable agreement is for the nonowned hospital to obtain a business associate agreement with the facility providing the information services.

As described in the HIPAA Privacy Rule, an OHCA is formed in order to share protected health information with members of the OHCA. The first type of OHCA arrangement can be formed when two or more legally separate covered entities provide service in a clinically integrated care setting. The classic example of this is the independent physician providing care in a hospital.

The second type of OHCA arrangement is one in which multiple covered entities participate in a joint arrangement, and together they contract or provide utilization review, quality assessment or improvement, or payment activities, the latter when the group as a whole shares the financial risk. Often, the public perceives this group of healthcare providers as participating in a joint arrangement. An example is the independent practice association formed by a large number of physicians who still retain their legal independence.

The whole point of these arrangements is to allow the sharing of protected health information compiled by any, or all, of the parties for the purpose of managing their joint operations. Without this ability to share information, each legally separate covered entity would have to obtain authorizations from each of his or her patients before sharing protected health information for the joint enterprise.

On the other hand, a business associate relationship is formed when a person or organization, which is not part of the covered entity's workforce, provides a service for or on behalf of a covered entity, which involves the need for the organization providing the service to have access to protected health information of the covered entity. In this case, there appears to be no common enterprise or benefit to a common enterprise. Instead, a service such as information technology is provided to another covered entity. It is possible for a covered entity to be a business associate of another covered entity, if it meets this definition.

References

Department of Health and Human Services. 2000. Final Rule: Standards for the Privacy of Individually Identifiable Health Information. *Federal Register* 65(250):82494; Department of Health and Human Services. 45 CFR §160.103.

Scenario 2

Should we restrict access of physicians to our electronic clinical record?

State and federal laws

KEY WORDS TO SEARCH: consent, authorization

Alcohol and substance abuse laws

Federal Drug and Alcohol Treatment Program Regulations require a signed authorization from a patient in order to disclose records to other treatment providers, except in emergency situations. Even in emergency situations, the information to be disclosed should be limited to the information necessary for the care.

The HIPAA Privacy Rule concept of "minimum necessary" does not apply to disclosures made for treatment purposes. However, the covered entity must define, within the organization, what information physicians need as part of their treatment role. Not all disclosures to physicians may be for treatment purposes.

Many covered entities have defaulted to full access for the physician's role. The writers of the Privacy Rule significantly revised the final wording of the minimum necessary standard upon receiving a large number of comments on this issue. The arguments were that to restrict access by physicians to information is contrary to sound medical practice, would increase medical errors, and would lead to increased liability. In many cases, the standard would not work in daily treatment situations and could be potentially dangerous to the patient. Critical information could be withheld if the facility imposed constraints as part of a minimum necessary standard.

Currently, there is no set of parameters to determine what information another caregiver will need for the proper diagnosis and treatment of a patient. Healthcare providers assert that they have an ethical duty to limit the sharing of unnecessary medical information. They have well-established practice standards in place and do not need a regulation to impose a standard in this case. A covered entity may rely on oral statements, written practice standards, medical staff bylaws, or confidentiality agreements to establish appropriate physician access.

Some covered entities do restrict access by physicians until they establish their identity and authority to use the information about new patients for treatment. Certain steps are followed to ensure proper access, such as calling an information systems department, or checking the reason for the access on an additional screen. However, care must be taken to ensure that these additional processes do not adversely impact the care of the patient.

References

Department of Health and Human Services. 45 CFR §§164.502, 164.514(d)(h); Department of Health and Human Services. 2000. Final Rule: Standards for the Privacy of Individually Identifiable Health Information. *Federal Register* 65(250): Commentary, § 164.514(d)—Minimum Necessary [CR 1]; 42 CFR §§ 2.13, 2.31, 2.51.

Scenario 3

If we provide transcription services in our facility for outside physicians, what privacy agreements apply?

Alcohol and substance abuse laws

Federal Drug and Alcohol Treatment Program Regulations permit the disclosure of information to an entity having direct administrative control over that program. If the transcription services are being provided for a program outside the facility, the facility should enter into a qualified service organization agreement with the Program.

If physicians are dictating information on patients they are treating in the facility, the disclosure of protected health information to the transcriptionists would be considered healthcare operations, and therefore, permitted under the HIPAA Privacy Rule.

If physicians are dictating information on their private patients, however, it would be necessary for the physicians to obtain a business associate agreement with the facility. It is permitted by the Privacy Rule for one covered entity to be a business associate of another covered entity. In this case, the facility becomes the physicians' business associate, because the facility is providing the service for the physicians. It would not be hard for the facility to meet the requirements of the business associate agreement, as the facility already meets these requirements as a covered entity.

The physicians and the facility are part of an Organized Health Care Arrangement (OHCA) if the physicians are treating patients at the facility. It is permitted for physicians to disclose protected health information to the facility for healthcare operations purposes of the OHCA. However, providing transcription services for private practice patients does not appear to be benefiting the arrangement, just the physicians. Therefore, the OHCA provisions alone would not be adequate to allow the physicians to disclose the protected health information to the facility.

References

Department of Health and Human Services. 45 CFR §§ 160.103, 164.502(e), 164.506(c).

Scenario 4

Does HIPAA define who owns a medical record or how long it must be retained?

 State and federal laws

KEY WORDS TO SEARCH: ownership of records, retention requirements, and statute of limitations

The HIPAA Privacy Rule does not address who owns the physical or electronic records of the covered entity. In the Privacy Rule, there is no right for an individual to obtain original records about themselves, but it does grant rights to patients to access and obtain copies of their designated records sets. In order to determine ownership of records, state law must be consulted. In most states, the originator of the documents, such as the healthcare facility or the healthcare provider, owns the physical records. The Privacy Rule also does not define how long records must be retained, except for documents related to compliance with the Privacy Rule, which is six years. Often, state or federal regulations define how long facilities or healthcare providers must retain original records. Statute of limitations timeframes also apply to how long records should be kept by healthcare providers. Even after a healthcare provider dies, the records of his or her practice are commonly considered part of the property of the provider's estate.

After the period of retention and statute of limitation timeframes are met, the healthcare provider may choose to destroy the records. However, as long as the records are maintained by the covered entity, the Privacy Rule protections still apply to the protected health information contained in them. Physical records can only be transferred to a person who is permitted to receive information by the HIPAA Privacy Rule. This could be either the individual to whom the records pertain, a personal representative of the individual, another covered entity, or a person who will become a covered entity, such as a newly licensed physician purchasing a retiring physician's practice.

Finally, some state laws also assign some ownership rights to the individual's medical record to the individual, but do not necessarily transfer the ownership solely to the individual.

References

Department of Health and Human Services. 45 CFR §§160.501, 164.530. Final Rule: Standards for the Privacy of Individually Identifiable Health Information. *Federal Register* 65(250): 12/28/2000 Commentary to the Privacy Rule, CR 4.

Scenario 5

When do we need a data use agreement?

The HIPAA Privacy Rule allows a covered entity to disclose what is called a "limited data set" for the purposes of research, public health, or healthcare operations. A limited data set does not include most of an individual's identifiers as listed in the safe harbor, de-identification method. However, unlike the de-identified data set, a limited data set may include dates related to an individual, as well as an individual's address details such as town or city, state, and zip code. The addition of these elements makes the data set much more usable for research, public health, or healthcare operations than a totally de-identified data set.

There are some benefits for both the covered entity and recipients of the limited data set. The covered entity does not have to account for the disclosure of this information. Researchers, although they may have to obtain approval for their research from an Institutional Review Board, would not have to make the additional certifications necessary to obtain a waiver of authorization for their research. An entity doing healthcare operations using the limited data set would not have to agree to a business associate agreement. A public health agency would not have to demonstrate that it has statutory authority or permission to obtain the data.

However, the Privacy Rule still considers this data set identifiable and in need of protection. In order to receive the limited data set, the researcher, public health agency, or provider of the healthcare operations service needs to agree to a different type of assurance that the information will be handled appropriately. This assurance is called a *data use agreement*. This type of agreement must establish the permitted use and disclosure of the information and restricts the recipient from using the data for other purposes. The recipient also agrees to use appropriate safeguards to prevent a non-permitted disclosure of the information, agrees to report to the covered entity if there is an inappropriate disclosure, and agrees to apply the same provisions to agents or subcontractors. Finally, and most importantly, the recipient agrees to not identify the information or contact the individuals. The covered entity may create the limited data set, or may engage a business associate to do so, prior to the disclosure.

The covered entity should consider the best way to ensure these agreements are obtained. If a covered entity does a great deal of research, the appropriate person to review and determine if data use agreements are needed may be a person who reviews and obtains other types of research-related agreements, or, this assignment may reside with the person who obtains business associate agreements.

The covered entity must ensure that it acts on any reported violations of a data use agreement. These actions are similar to the actions required when a business associate is in violation of the business associate agreement. The covered entity has an obligation to demand the recipient of the data set cure the problem. If the problem is not fixed, the covered entity should discontinue any disclosure of the limited data set and report the problem to the Secretary of the Department of Health and Human Services.

References

Department of Health and Human Services. 45 CFR §§ 164.512(i), 164.514(a), (e).

Scenario 6

What happens if we fail to initiate a business associate agreement with someone who meets the definition of a business associate?

A covered entity may only use or disclose protected health information as permitted or required by the HIPAA Privacy Rule. Outside of the disclosures required, permitted by law, or authorized by the patient, the only way a covered entity is permitted to disclose protected health information to a noncovered entity, or permit a noncovered entity to receive protected health information on its behalf, is to have a business associate agreement with the party who will receive the protected health information.

A business associate agreement provides assurance to the covered entity that the noncovered entity will safeguard the protected health information. The only time the obligation to obtain a business associate agreement does not apply is when the disclosure is to another healthcare provider who may not be a covered entity, but even then the disclosure must be for the purpose of treatment, payment of treatment, or limited healthcare operations purposes. These limited disclosures for the healthcare operations of the noncovered treatment provider must only be for assessing quality and improvement, evaluating outcomes of care, developing clinical guidelines, coordinating care or case management, providing treatment alternatives, developing treatment protocols, credentialing, or assessing the practitioner performance; training of students, trainees, or practitioners in health care; or population-focused activities intended to improve care or reduce costs. In these cases, the information shared with the noncovered treatment provider must be about a patient that both entities are treating. There are also some exceptions for group health plan disclosures to plan sponsors and for government programs for certain activities.

When the situation requires a business associate agreement, and the covered entity does not obtain one, the covered entity is violating the standards of the Privacy Rule in the following ways: First, by not obtaining the required agreement, and, second, violating the standards every time the covered entity discloses protected health information to the noncovered entity. Further, if the noncovered entity does something that is a violation of the Privacy Rule, the covered entity can be held responsible for the civil money penalty, if any. If a noncovered entity refuses to agree to the business associate agreement as provided by the Privacy Rule, the covered entity should seek a different provider for the service.

References

Department of Health and Human Services. 45 CFR §§ 160.402(c), 164.502(e)(1), 164.504(e).

Scenario 7

What should we do when we terminate a business associate who no longer works on our organization's behalf?

The HIPAA Privacy Rule requires the covered entity to take certain actions when a business associate relationship is terminated. Upon notice of the termination, the covered entity needs to contact the business associate and determine if the entity still retains any protected health information from, or created for, the covered entity.

The protected health information must be destroyed, returned to the covered entity, or transferred to another business associate. If the information cannot be destroyed, but must be maintained by the business associate for legal or retention regulations, then the safeguards of the contract must be extended. An existing business associate agreement can be amended or a new one created, stating the limitations of uses and disclosures of the protected health information and the reason the return or destruction of the information is not feasible. If the information is to be transferred, the covered entity should inform the business associate that the contract extends until all of the information is transferred. If the protected health information is to be destroyed, the covered entity should ask the business associate to destroy the information in a way that does not allow the identifiable information to be retrieved. If the information is electronic and needs to be transferred, the covered entity should ensure that the information transfer is accomplished in a secure fashion.

Once the protected health information is transferred or destroyed, it is recommended that the covered entity obtain a certification from the business associate that either it has no protected health information, or all protected health information it had in its possession, or in the possession of any of its agents or subcontractors, has been destroyed or returned to the covered entity.

Finally, if the business associate has disclosed any information that needed to be included in an accounting of disclosures, or performed any other activity that generated documentation required by the Privacy Rule, the business associate is required to maintain the documentation for six years after the date of the action. Alternatively, the business associate can also return this information to the covered entity. The latter is probably the best practice, because the covered entity generally has a process to store and retrieve these documents when a patient requests an accounting of disclosures.

The covered entity should retain business associate agreements and termination-related correspondence for six years from the date of termination.

If the business associate is required by law to perform certain functions, other constraints may apply. The business associate, often a government agency, may be required to retain the information. The original business associate agreement, or memorandum of understanding, should state this, so no further action on the part of the covered entity is required to destroy or retrieve protected health information.

Finally, if a business associate is terminated and refuses to return the protected health information, it is in violation of the business associate agreement. Legal counsel should be consulted to determine if there are actions that should be taken. The covered entity should report the refusal to comply with the business associate agreement to the Secretary of Health and Human Services.

References

Department of Health and Human Services. 45 CFR §§ 164.312, 164.314, 164.504(e), 164.530(j).

Scenario 8

May we allow outside vendors to take photos of our newborns?

The first question the facility needs to answer is whether this is an appropriate activity that relates to the primary function of the covered entity. Each facility must determine if this activity is part of the treatment of the mother, or if it relates to a healthcare operations purpose for the facility. Some facilities have justified this photography as a safety measure, to assist in identifying the newborn.

Determining the purpose of this activity is important because it drives the question of whether the use of protected health information, such as mother's name, location, and delivery, is an appropriate use of the information under the HIPAA Privacy Rule. If this activity is not considered a treatment or healthcare operations activity, then an authorization to disclose the information, even to facility staff or volunteers for this purpose, is necessary.

If a vendor is performing this function, once again, it is important to know the purpose of the activity. When a vendor is involved, often the scope of the activity may go well beyond the covered functions of the healthcare provider. It would be hard to justify a business associate agreement if the vendor was selling photograph copies or posting the pictures on a secure web site for out-of-area families to view. In that case, the vendor is really not providing a service for or on behalf of the covered entity, and it would be hard to justify a business associate agreement. If the vendor is not involved in the covered functions of the facility, then the activity of producing the photograph is not covered by the Privacy Rule. Because the vendor is not a covered entity, the facility should communicate clearly to the mother that the vendor is not acting for the facility in providing this service.

There are additional considerations, however, for the facility which involve the Privacy Rule. How does the vendor know who the new mothers are and their location in the facility? The Privacy Rule allows the facility to provide the location of a patient who has not opted out of the facility directory to visitors, only if the visitor knows the patient's name. A vendor would not be expected to be aware of the patient's name. Allowing the vendor to view a census list of the obstetrical floor, or notifying the vendor of a birth, would be considered a violation of the Privacy Rule, as this disclosure is not permitted or required by the Rule.

The only way a vendor should be provided this information is by an authorization signed by the mother or a person with legal authority to act on behalf of the child. A staff member or the facility can alert the mother to this service, provide an authorization, and communicate with the vendor once the authorization is signed. Otherwise, the mother's information should not be provided to a vendor. Once an authorization is signed, however, the vendor can be given information about the location of the mother.

References

Department of Health and Human Services. 2000. 45 CFR §160.103, 164.510(a)(i), 164.502(a)

Scenario 9

Are long-term care insurers required to follow the HIPAA Privacy Rule?

Some long-term care plans are under the HIPAA Privacy Rule, and some are not. If the plan is a nursing home fixed indemnity policy and limited to payments made solely for nursing facility care, then this type of plan is not considered a health plan in regards to the HIPAA Privacy, Security or Transactions Rules. Therefore, those companies that issue only these types of policies would not be covered entities.

However, more comprehensive long-term care policies are considered health plans under the Privacy Rule. Therefore, the issuers of these types of long-term care policies are considered to be covered entities. If the covered entity who issues these policies offers both fixed indemnity and more comprehensive long-term care policies, the covered entity must decide whether to follow the Privacy Rule for the fixed indemnity policies, or whether it wishes to be considered a hybrid entity and exclude the fixed indemnity policy portion of its business from the requirement of the Privacy Rule.

References

Department of Health and Human Services. 2000. Final Rule: Standards for the Privacy of Individually Identifiable Health Information. *Federal Register* 65(250):82578; Department of Health and Human Services. 45 CFR §160.103; The Health Insurance Portability and Accountability Act, Section 1171(5)(G).

Scenario 10

Do we have to meet the HIPAA Privacy Rule when conducting a health fair?

In general, the HIPAA Privacy Rule applies to activities in which a covered entity creates or receives individually identifiable health information relative to the physical health or condition of an individual. If and to what extent the Privacy Rule applies to health fair activities depends on the extent of services provided at the health fair.

Health fairs often do not collect information on the individuals who attend, and when they have a sign-in sheet, it is used for prizes or future promotions. In either of these cases, there is no identifiable information, or the identifiable information is collected for a purpose unrelated to treatment. Therefore, the Privacy Rule requirements do not apply.

If the list of individuals who signed up for promotional material includes not only contact information but also disease information, or the list is matched up with the individual's protected health information maintained by the covered entity, and the covered entity intends on using it to contact the individuals to promote certain products or services, then it may come under the provisions of the Privacy Rule. Careful analysis should be made to determine whether the individual permits the planned use of this information by the covered entity without his or her authorization.

If the healthcare provider also does screening tests as part of the health fair, much depends on the test results being identifiable. If the individual's identity is not recorded and the individual is merely given the results of the test, then, no identifiable information is created or received, and the Privacy Rule does not apply.

However, if the healthcare provider records and maintains the identifiable results, for example, so as to provide the results to the individual's family physician or to use the information to assist the individual in finding an appropriate physician to provide care, then the Privacy Rule provisions would apply. In this case, it may be considered that the healthcare provider is providing treatment services, and the healthcare provider may have to offer a Notice of Privacy Practices to the individual.

References

Department of Health and Human Services. 45 CFR §§160.103, 164.501, 164.520.

Scenario 11

Should we follow the HIPAA Privacy Rule when conducting a flu shot clinic?

The HIPAA Privacy Rule applies to covered entities and to activities of covered entities when they create or receive individually identifiable health information relative to the physical health or condition of an individual. Applications of the Privacy Rule to a flu shot clinic depend on: First, whether a covered entity is providing the service; second, the extent of the records generated by the activity.

Many times, public health departments provide flu shot clinics. A public health department may not be a covered entity. It depends on whether the department provides treatment services, and if so, how it is reimbursed for treatment services. If the public health department is not a covered entity, or if the flu shot clinic is being conducted by a noncovered entity, such as an employer, this activity is not under the Privacy Rule.

However, if the public health department is a covered entity, or if a covered healthcare provider conducts the flu shot clinic, then, the next question is if the activity involves the generation of identifiable records. If the covered entity maintains the identifiable results, for example, noting them in a patient's clinic record, then the Privacy Rule provisions would apply. A Notice of Privacy Practices for the covered entity should be provided to the individual if this is the first time services have been provided to the individual.

Finally, if a covered healthcare provider is conducting a flu shot clinic for its employees, as part of an employee health initiative, the activity is considered an employee health activity and any records generated should be filed with the employee health record. As long as the activity is performed at the direction of the employer, and any records are used only for employment purposes, these activities would not be under the Privacy Rule.

References

Department of Health and Human Services. 45 CFR §§160.103, 164.520.

Scenario 12

How does HIPAA apply to vendors of medical devices or pharmaceuticals that come to our facility?

The HIPAA Privacy Rule does not address vendors who are nonworkforce individuals often found in healthcare facilities. The reason these individuals, usually vendors of medical devices or pharmaceuticals, are present in the facility can vary widely.

The covered entity needs to challenge the reason each of these vendors is in the facility and the extent to which the vendor should have access to protected health information. It is the facility's responsibility to safeguard the privacy of patients, so it is up to the covered entity to decide to what extent these individuals may be present in the healthcare setting. At a minimum, a consistently-used process to identify these individuals should be established, and identifiers, such as badges, used to clearly distinguish them from employees. Rules of acceptable vendor behavior should be established related to interactions with patients, locations where vendors are permitted within the facility, and sanctions should the vendors disregard these rules. As these vendors are not part of the workforces of the covered entity, the covered entity does not have the responsibility to provide Privacy Rule requirements training. However, it may be good practice to provide a vendor orientation that covers patient privacy expectations.

Pharmaceutical salespeople are in the healthcare facility to communicate information about products or to provide samples to healthcare providers and pharmacists. Pharmaceutical salespeople do not need access to protected health information, nor should they be allowed access to this information. Their exposure to protected health information can be considered an incidental exposure, and the covered entity should take reasonable precautions to keep that exposure as limited as possible.

If a vendor needs to be present to provide just-in-time education to a healthcare provider and needs access to protected health information to provide this service, then an authorization from the patient may be required. A recurring educational relationship may warrant a business associate agreement.

If vendors are providing Food and Drug Administration (FDA) regulated products, then they may be provided protected health information about the FDA-regulated product, but it should be limited to the information necessary for the company's reporting requirements.

Finally, when vendors are actively involved in providing treatment, such as measuring and providing prosthetic devices, they may be considered noncovered treatment providers and receive protected health information necessary for the treatment. Healthcare providers need to be very careful, however, that they do not provide protected health information to vendors for marketing purposes without authorization from patients.

References

Department of Health and Human Services. 45 CFR §§164.508(a)(3), 164.512(b), 164.530 (c); Department of Health and Human Services. 2000. Final Rule: Standards for the Privacy of Individually Identifiable Health Information. *Federal Register* 65(250):82569.

SECTION II

Reducing Incidental Disclosures
with Reasonable Safeguards

This section discusses common activities in clinical areas that may result in incidental disclosure of protected health information. It suggests best practices to reduce these incidental disclosures but still allow the communication necessary for the healthcare provider to continue. It also articulates privacy concerns that should be addressed with new technologies.

Scenario 13

Are "White Boards," erasable patient information boards, allowed in HIPAA?

White boards, erasable patient information boards, are a means of communicating certain information about patients to the healthcare providers who care for them. One use is a board that has patient safety-related information about an individual patient. This information might include fall precautions, transfer status, and difficulty in swallowing: important information for a healthcare provider to know. The HIPAA Privacy Rule repeatedly states that the intent of the Rule is not to interfere with customary and necessary communications in the healthcare of the individual. In this case, the safety of the patient comes first.

This information should be limited to the minimum necessary for the purpose, and the board should be posted in a designated area to reduce disclosures to individuals who are not involved in the care of the patient, such as to visitors to the patient's room. Visitors may see this information on a board posted in the patient's room, but often these visitors are family or friends who have been invited by the patient; therefore, the healthcare provider can assume the patient is comfortable with the visitors seeing the information. The patient should be informed of the right to deny access to any "well meaning, but intrusive visitors." Some providers use symbols known only to the healthcare providers to communicate the information.

A second type of board may have multiple patients' information listed. It is used by healthcare providers to monitor the current status and location of patients in areas where the patients' status or location is frequently changing. This type of board may be effectively used in an emergency or obstetrical department. Each facility needs to assess the use of these status boards based on certain criteria:

- Is the board essential to the communication in the department?
- Does the board's presence add to the safe and efficient treatment of the patients involved?
- Is the information about the patient limited to the minimum for the purpose?
- Can initials be used instead of names?
- Can room numbers be used instead of names?
- Are all of the critical elements and required data listed and displayed in a manner that is useful for the healthcare providers?
- Is the board located in the best location to reduce incidental disclosures, but out of the site lines of the public?
- Finally, have other options been explored that might function just as well?

It is recommended that the answers to these questions be documented by the facility. It is valuable that someone knowledgeable of the Privacy Rule, such as the facility privacy official, assess the use. The facility should also reassess the use of these boards periodically to see that the above criteria are still being met.

References

Department of Health and Human Services, 2000. 45 CFR §164.530(c)(2); Department of Health and Human Services, Office for Civil Rights. 2003. Incidental Disclosures. Available online from http://www.dhhs.gov/ocr/hipaa/guidelines/incidentalud.pdf; Department of Health and Human Services, Office for Civil Rights. Your Frequently Asked Questions On Privacy. Available online from http://www.dhhs.gov/ocr/hipaa/.

Scenario 14

What can be done to protect privacy in semiprivate rooms?

The HIPAA Privacy Rule allows communications to occur for treatment purposes and between healthcare providers and patients. The preamble repeatedly states the intent of the Rule is not to interfere with customary and necessary communications for the healthcare of the individual. However, the writers of the Rule also recognized that there are situations in which incidental disclosures cannot be reduced.

Many suggestions have been presented with the goal of increasing the patient's privacy in semiprivate rooms, such as using TV or radio static to muffle conversations, keeping voices as low as possible, or hanging sound muffling curtains. However, background static or low voices may also prevent the patient from hearing information needed to make critical health discussions. There is often very little space in these rooms, especially when treatment-related machines, walkers, and other treatment paraphernalia for two patients are added to the room. Sometimes, the healthcare provider does not have enough room to pull the curtain far enough to maintain privacy during discussions. Of course, the provider can ask the other patient's visitors to leave the room, so at least the visitors do not hear the discussions. As it is nearly impossible to maintain privacy in these rooms, this was one reason why incidental disclosures are not considered violations of the Privacy Rule.

References

Department of Health and Human Services. 45. CFR §164.530(c)(2); Department of Health and Human Services, Office for Civil Rights. Your Frequently Asked Questions On Privacy. Available online from http://www.dhhs.gov/ocr/hipaa/.

Scenario 15

Is calling out a patient name in a waiting room permitted by HIPAA?

Alcohol and substance abuse laws

Drug and Alcohol Treatment Program Federal Record Regulations permit the disclosure of a patient's name only by authorization, court order, or if it is not used in connection with the fact that the patient is receiving drug or alcohol treatment services.

The HIPAA Privacy Rule allows communications to occur for treatment purposes. The preamble repeatedly states the intent of the Rule is not to interfere with customary and necessary communications in the healthcare of the individual. Calling out a patient's name in a waiting room, or even on the facility's paging system, is considered an incidental disclosure, and therefore, allowed in the Privacy Rule.

However, during those communications, the healthcare provider must take reasonable precautions that the information is limited to the minimum necessary for the purpose. For example, the healthcare provider should not announce, "Mr. Patient, the result of your cholesterol test is . . . ." in a public waiting room. This would be considered a violation of the minimum necessary standards of the Privacy Rule.

Some providers attempt to limit the disclosure by announcing only the first name of the patient. However, there may be circumstances unrelated to the Privacy Rule that might discourage handling the issue this way, such as the patient perceiving a lack of respect with this practice. There is also the remote risk that the wrong patient responds to the summons by first name.

Although there is no violation in announcing a patient name in the Privacy Rule, it is good practice to consider ways to reduce the patient's perception that his or her privacy has been violated by the practice. Some suggestions are:

- ◆ Be as efficient as possible in scheduling appointments so waiting time is minimized.

- ◆ Provide opportunities for patients to complete forms prior to appointment time, such as utilizing online access to forms, so their wait is minimized.

- ◆ Provide feedback to architects about privacy concerns as facilities are being built or remodeled.

- ◆ Expand the facilities in areas where there is a high volume for a particular service, resulting in crowded waiting rooms.

- ◆ Consider using more technology, such as more efficient electronic appointment systems, flashing pagers, such as those used for restaurant lines, or even text messages directed to the patient's mobile phone.

References

Department of Health and Human Services. 45 CFR §164.530(c)(2); Department of Health and Human Services, Office for Civil Rights. 2003. Incidental Disclosures. Available online from http://www.dhhs.gov/ocr/hipaa/guidelines/incidentalud.pdf; Department of Health and Human Services, Office for Civil Rights. Your Frequently Asked Questions On Privacy. Available online from http://www.dhhs.gov/ocr/hipaa/; Department of Health and Human Services. 42 CFR § 2.2(a).

Scenario 16

Can we use "job-shadowing" of our employees and still be in compliance with HIPAA?

 Alcohol and substance abuse laws
Drug and Alcohol Treatment Programs are too protective of patient information privacy to permit this kind of activity.

Job-shadowing, "Take Your Child to Work Day," and allowing prospective medical school students to observe in healthcare settings, are activities that healthcare providers have undertaken to encourage individuals to consider healthcare-related professions. When these activities can be limited to areas in which the likelihood of exposure to protected health information is very limited, such as in administrative areas, they may be permitted. However, most of the time, these activities increase the risk of disclosures of protected health information beyond those considered "incidental," and have definite HIPAA Privacy Rule implications.

There is a provision in the Privacy Rule that permits students and trainees to practice and improve their skills in the healthcare environment, with the understanding that these students must have access to protected health information to do so. However, the context of this provision appears to imply that the students are already enrolled in a healthcare field of study and that they are under the supervision of the covered entity. Unfortunately, job-shadowing activities do not appear to apply in this exception.

The only other area this may be permitted is when these individuals can be considered "volunteers," such as those in work-study programs. The Privacy Rule treats volunteers as workforce, and the covered entity is responsible for their actions. In these cases, the covered entity must have direct control over volunteers. A volunteer, as with every other member of the covered entity's workforce, must be trained on the confidentiality and other requirements of the Privacy Rule. Some providers take the opportunity to train these students not only on HIPAA, but also on safety, dress code, name badge, hazardous chemicals, blood borne pathogens, and infection control procedures.

The other Privacy Rule consideration is the extent to which these volunteers need access to protected health information. As their "role" is to perform work-study, they should be allowed direct access to protected health information only as needed as part of their work-study assignment.

References

Department of Health and Human Services. 45 CFR §§164.506(b)(4), 160.103, 164.530(b), 164.514(2); Department of Health and Human Services. 42 CFR § 2.1; Davis, N., A. Halpert, B. Herrin, and C. Lemery. Job shadowing and the HIPAA Privacy Rule. *Journal of American Health Information Management Association* 77, 8:69, 71.

Scenario 17

Can patients continue to sign in for appointments?

Alcohol and substance abuse laws

Drug and Alcohol Treatment Program Federal Record Regulations permit the disclosure of a patient's name as long it is not used in connection with the fact that the patient is receiving drug or alcohol treatment services. If a program shares a waiting room with other providers, a sign-in log would be permitted if the patient did not have to indicate he or she was there for program services.

The HIPAA Privacy Rule allows communications to occur for treatment purposes. The preamble repeatedly states the intent of the Rule was not to interfere with customary and necessary communications for the healthcare of the individual. Patients may sign their names on a waiting room list, and if another patient sees it, that is considered an incidental disclosure.

However, in determining the content of these sign-in lists, the healthcare provider must take reasonable precautions that the information is limited to the minimum necessary for the purpose. For example, the healthcare provider should not ask patients to also write the reason for their visit or whether they have health insurance.

Some providers have attempted to limit the disclosure by having patients sign in on a label sheet, which allows their names to be removed as soon as they are registered.

References

Department of Health and Human Services. 45 CFR §164.530(c)(2); Department of Health and Human Services. 42 CFR § 2.1; Department of Health and Human Services, Office for Civil Rights. 2003. Incidental Disclosures. Available online from http://www.dhhs.gov/ocr/hipaa/guidelines/incidentalud.pdf/.

Scenario 18

What is a good way to dispose of items, such as specimen cups and IV bags, that have protected health information (PHI) on them?

The HIPAA Privacy Rule requires covered entities to take reasonable precautions to safeguard protected health information when it is used for treatment, payment, or healthcare operations. It is critical for patient care and safety that certain items be labeled with the patient's identity. Labeling these items with identifiable information is considered a part of treatment.

When the question of shredding prescription vials as a requirement of the Privacy Rule arose, the Office for Civil Rights, in its published guidance documents, initially answered in the negative. However, shredding protected health information on paper appears to be a reasonable safeguard to meet this section of the regulation. In an effort to meet this requirement, covered entities have realized that it is not only paper or electronic records that contain protected health information. Other by-products of the treatment process have individually identifiable information as well.

There are four common methods used by healthcare facilities to destroy the protected health information on specimen cups, IV bags, and similar items. These are to: use permanent markers to mark out the protected health information before discarding the item in the regular trash; remove the labels and place the labels in confidential trash to be shredded; place the items in biohazard trash; or place special labels over the protected health information prior to disposal.

When a covered entity is deciding on a method of de-identifying these items for disposal, it is important that the choice of a safeguard be reasonable. The probability of risk of disclosure based on a person retrieving one of these identifiable items should be balanced against the cost and effort to de-identify the item. The covered entity may find that placing such items in biohazard bags is extremely expensive because of the additional cost to pay for the destruction of these items. The facility needs to consider the time it takes for a nurse to place special labels to cover the patient's name and decide whether this activity is a good use of skilled, highly-paid personnel.

References

Department of Health and Human Services. 45 CFR §164.530(c); Department of Health and Human Services, Office for Civil Rights. 2001. Minimum Necessary. No longer available in this version online from http://www.dhhs.gov/ocr/hipaa/guidelines/incidentalud.pdf/.

Scenario 19

Are privacy screens on PCs a good idea?

The HIPAA Privacy Rule requires covered entities to provide reasonable safeguards to prevent incidental disclosures. Incidental disclosures are considered the unintentional communications of individually identifiable information to a person who should not see or hear the information.

A privacy screen on a PC is a good option when the covered entity has employees located in areas where the public may see the contents of the screen while the screen has individually identifiable information displayed on it. Privacy screens are useful in common areas such as reception areas, admitting areas, or open nursing stations. However, the Privacy Rule requires that covered entities make reasonable efforts to meet this standard. Requiring these screens on all PCs, even in areas restricted from the public, may be expensive and not reasonable.

Password protected screensavers set to activate after a period of time, VESA standard display mounting equipment, or doors to cover the screen when not actively in use are other options to consider.

References

Department of Health and Human Services. 45 CFR §164.530(c)(2).

Scenario 20

Is it okay to communicate health information using messaging service software?

The HIPAA Privacy Rule does not address the use of this type of software, other than the general statement that the covered entity must provide reasonable safeguards to protect individually identifiable information. However, the HIPAA Security Rule would require that the risks to security and privacy be assessed with the use of any software product used by the covered entity.

Setting aside other security considerations, the main threat to privacy in using messaging service software is that protected health information can be transmitted outside of the covered entity using messaging services. Not only may an inappropriate disclosure be made, but transmitting messages using this software is not very secure and can be easily breached. It is possible to install monitoring and filtering software, but this is difficult and certainly not something a covered entity can depend on to adequately protect the covered entity from inappropriate disclosures. Managers at the department level can monitor workforce use. However, this may not be a practical approach.

The covered entity has the responsibility to implement policies and procedures to address the disclosure of protected health information. Limitations of use or nonuse of this type of software should be addressed in policies about secure transmission of protected health information, as well as in policies outlining when disclosure of protected health information is permitted. The covered entity also has the responsibility to educate the workforce on those policies and to sanction a member of the workforce should they violate the policy or regulations regarding the disclosure of protected health information.

If the covered entity determines that the use of messaging services is a high risk to the privacy and security of the institution, and there is difficulty monitoring its use, they should not permit its use by the workforce.

References

Department of Health and Human Services. 45 CFR §§164.308, 164.530 (b), (c), (e); Sterneckert, A. 2003. *Critical Incident Management.* Boca Raton: Auerbach Publications, 385.

Scenario 21

Should a physician be able to access an electronic health record at home?

The HIPAA Privacy Rule permits healthcare providers to access protected health information for treatment purposes. However, there is also a requirement that the covered entity provide reasonable safeguards to protect the information. Further, the HIPAA Security Rule requires a covered entity to:

- Ensure the confidentiality, integrity, and availability of all electronically protected health information the covered entity creates, receives, maintains, or transmits
- Protect against any reasonably anticipated threats or hazards to the security or integrity of such information
- Protect against any reasonably anticipated uses or disclosures of such information that are not permitted or required
- Ensure compliance by its workforce

These requirements are not easy to meet when the access is from an unsecured location. In addition, if the physician has access and can print or copy the information, it further increases the possibility of a violation of the regulations.

However, proper technology can mitigate some of the risks. Physicians can gain access via a dedicated portal on a secure gateway or have Virtual Private Network (VPN) access. This goes a long way to protect the security of the delivery method. These portals can be configured so that any printing will not include the header information containing the identity of the patient. The covered entity is responsible for the electronic record and must evaluate the benefits to patient treatment and the increased security of the physician against the risks to patient privacy.

Finally, it is worth noting that if the physician is a separate covered entity, the physician has the responsibility to meet the same HIPAA privacy and security standards as the covered entity that creates and maintains the records. In this circumstance, the covered entity that provides the electronic access may require a physician to sign an agreement that, in return for the privilege of accessing the health record from home, he or she will provide reasonable safeguards to protect the information.

References

Department of Health and Human Services. 45 CFR § §164.306, 164.506, 164.530(c).

Scenario 22

What privacy risks should be considered with the use of Web cameras?

Web camera technology provides new opportunities for family members to stay involved in the care of a patient, even when the family is not living nearby. This technology allows the family to communicate with the patient at any time during the patient's stay. When the patient is a child, it allows a parent who may need to care for siblings to still be involved in the child's care. Finally, it may be a preferable method for a family to visit when the patient is immunocompromised.

The first consideration is whether the Internet access and equipment will be provided by the patient's family or by the facility. If provided by the family, there is no requirement for them to be compliant with the HIPAA Security Rule, as they are not covered entities. In order for the families to provide this service, the facility must permit cell phone use within the facility. Use of family-owned equipment may be the simplest solution for the covered entity because it eliminates the technology required for a HIPAA Security Rule transmission.

However, privacy issues still remain. The HIPAA Privacy Rule does not address the use of Web cameras. Such technology was probably not even considered at the time the regulation was written. However, there is the requirement that the covered entity provide reasonable safeguards to protect the privacy of a patient's information, which can include a patient's image. When the patient is in a semiprivate room, the chances of breaching another patient's privacy is probably too great to allow the Web camera option. The patient needs to understand that use of the Webcam is a privilege, not a right. If privacy issues are raised, the facility will have the right to ask the family to discontinue the camera's use. It is desirable for the patient to sign a special consent that allows the use of the Webcam and also describes the conditions for the Webcam use.

References

Department of Health and Human Services. 45 CFR §164.530(c).

Scenario 23

Are we allowed to display babies' names on their cribs in the nursery?

Displaying the name on a crib may be considered a permitted communication of individually identifiable information for treatment purposes. The preamble of the HIPAA Privacy Rule repeatedly states the intent of the Rule is not to interfere with customary and necessary communications for the healthcare of the individual. Often, this is a patient safety issue to ensure that a baby is properly identified.

However, in making these communications, the healthcare provider must take reasonable precautions that the information is limited to the minimum necessary for the purpose. Having too much information available that could potentially be seen by visitors in a newborn viewing area may raise other infant safety concerns.

A good solution is to have two cards on the crib. One, viewable to visitors, may contain minimal information such as whether the baby is a girl or a boy, the mother's room number, and the pediatrician's name. The other card would be viewable only to staff and would contain the baby's name, weight, birth date, or other information needed by the staff.

References

Department of Health and Human Services. 45 CFR §164.530(c)(2); Department of Health and Human Services, Office for Civil Rights. 2003. Incidental Disclosures. Available online from http://www.dhhs.gov/ocr/hipaa/guidelines/incidentalud.pdf/; Department of Health and Human Services, Office for Civil Rights. Your Frequently Asked Questions On Privacy. 202. Available online from http://www.dhhs.gov/ocr/hipaa/.

Scenario 24

Does HIPAA define where a fax machine should be placed in a facility?

Neither the HIPAA Privacy Rule nor the HIPAA Security Rule is so specific as to state where a fax machine should be located. The Privacy Rule states that a covered entity must safeguard protected health information and take reasonable steps to do so. The Security Rule does not even apply to faxed information, as facsimiles are generally not considered electronically protected health information unless the fax is computer to computer. In order to safeguard protected health information, a covered entity should use common sense and the best security practices to determine where to place fax machines or copiers that receive faxes.

Fax machines should be placed where they are convenient for staff, but not where the information can be viewed or retrieved by unauthorized persons. Faxed material should not be left unattended for long periods of time. A fax machine should be in a secure area. If used by several departments, unique mailboxes should be designated for each department so that the faxes can be stored but not printed until an authorized person does so.

A covered entity should provide guidelines for its workforce on when faxing information is permitted, as the risk of accidental disclosure is greater when using a fax than when using mail. The outgoing fax should include a cover sheet with a number to call should the fax be misdirected. Automatic fax systems should be routinely audited to ensure that the numbers are accurate.

References

Department of Health and Human Services. 45 CFR §§164.302, 164.530(c)(2).

SECTION III

It's the Law

This section highlights areas of interaction between state laws and the HIPAA Privacy Rule, in which the state law usually takes precedence if it offers greater privacy rights. It also covers complicated law enforcement-related situations, public health scenarios, and issues relating to subpoenas.

Scenario 25

When do we follow state law instead of HIPAA in requiring an authorization for treatment disclosures?

 State and federal laws

KEY WORDS TO SEARCH: consent, authorization, and disclosure

 Alcohol and substance abuse laws

Federal Drug and Alcohol Treatment Program Record Regulations require signing a consent or authorization for treatment disclosures outside the program, except in emergencies.

The HIPAA Privacy Rule sets minimum standards for patient information privacy. Some states have set higher or more protective privacy standards for health information disclosures, especially when records related to specific conditions such as mental health or HIV/AIDS are requested. A higher standard is set when the law is more protective of a patient's privacy. In this case, it is a higher standard to require the patient to control the disclosure of records, even for treatment.

Either federal law, such as the Drug and Alcohol Treatment Program Regulations, or state law can establish a higher standard that is more protective of a patient's privacy than the Privacy Rule. The higher standard must be followed instead of the Privacy Rule, unless it is in direct conflict with the Rule. If, for example, a state law requires patient authorization in order to permit a disclosure to the Secretary of the Department of Health and Human Services, this would be in conflict with the express terms of the Privacy Rule, even though the requirement of an authorization would be more protective of the patient's privacy rights.

Therefore, if state law requires patient authorization for treatment-related disclosures, the facility must obtain one. When a disclosure is requested from a facility in a different state, the state's laws where the facility possessing the information is located must be followed. Finally, if this is an emergency situation, some states that require authorizations may provide other options for the disclosure when the patient is unable to sign an authorization. Talk with the privacy official at the site; he or she should be able to cite the laws involved.

References

Department of Health and Human Services. 45 CFR §160.202.

Scenario 26

How do we know when to follow state or other laws instead of HIPAA?

State and federal laws

KEY WORDS TO SEARCH: consent, authorization, disclosure of health information, HIV/AIDS, minors, custody, executor, genetic test results, required reporting by healthcare providers, public health, worker's compensation, duty to warn, trauma, injury, and victim

Alcohol and substance abuse laws

Federal Drug and Alcohol Treatment Program Record Regulations are more protective of privacy than the HIPAA Privacy Rule. When HIPAA adds additional privacy protections, the business associate agreements are required in addition to qualified service organization agreements, and both regulations will need to be met.

The HIPAA Privacy Rule does not pre-empt state or other laws regarding the privacy of health records or access to an individual's health records except in certain situations. The Privacy Rule was intended to set a baseline of protections and rights for individuals. Therefore, any laws or regulations that afforded less protection than the Privacy Rule or threw more roadblocks in the way of individuals' rights to their records were pre-empted by HIPAA.

On the other hand, some states provide higher protections for certain types of records. If state laws require consent or authorization to disclose certain disease information, or make it easier for individuals to obtain their own information, such as requiring the covered entity to supply access to requested information sooner than the Privacy Rule states, then these state law must be followed.

Finally, the Privacy Rule defers to state laws in some areas. Examples would be state laws that govern minors' and parents' rights in healthcare, assignment of a deceased individual's personal representative, and workers' compensation activities.

The pre-emption analysis of state and other federal laws and regulations is a line-by-line effort. Although many states' laws were reviewed for pre-emption prior to the implementation date of the Privacy Rule, some analyses were cursory. Further, state laws are constantly changing and new laws being added, so pre-emption analysis is a never-ending process. Also, experience has shown that there are conflicts between some federal laws and regulations and the Privacy Rule; some federal agencies have issued clarifications in this regard.

One of the most challenging sections in the Privacy Rule regarding state and other federal law pre-emption is the section that deals with uses and disclosures for which an authorization or opportunity to agree or object is not required. When law enforcement disclosures are being considered, it is essential to determine if the disclosure is mandatory under state or federal law, or merely "permitted." If the reporting in state or federal law is permitted, but not required, the Privacy Rule needs to also have a provision that permits the reporting. If the Privacy Rule does not also permit the disclosure, the facility should only disclose the information if presented with an authorization, court order, subpoena, or other valid legal process. Wording which indicates permissive reporting is "may report; is permitted; is not considered privileged; if the provider, in their professional judgment . . ." as opposed to "providers must or shall report . . ." which would indicate required reporting.

Legal counsel should be consulted in situations where the facility is unsure of the requirements and authority of state or other federal laws.

References

Department of Health and Human Services. 45 CFR § §160.202, 164.512.

Scenario 27

Can we notify law enforcement when patients are discharged?

 State and federal laws

KEY WORDS TO SEARCH: law enforcement notification, required reporting of victims of crimes, suspect, fugitive, missing person, duty to report by healthcare providers, reporting of outstanding warrants, consent, and authorization

 Alcohol and substance abuse laws
Federal Drug and Alcohol Treatment Program Regulations require a patient's signed authorization to allow disclosure of records to law enforcement, unless there is a court order that permits such disclosures.

It is important to analyze state laws to determine what circumstances require healthcare providers to report to law enforcement. If the state law requires a healthcare provider to notify law enforcement in certain situations, such as when a patient has a gunshot wound, then the HIPAA Privacy Rule permits such a disclosure. However, the healthcare provider must only disclose the information the state law says to report, even though the Privacy Rule may allow more information to be given to law enforcement.

Many situations are not covered in required reporting laws, however. Law enforcement officers may be investigating a crime, discover that the suspect was injured, and believe that the suspect will be seeking care in a local facility. Another situation is when a confused patient is brought to the facility for care, and the family files a missing person report because they do not know where the individual has gone. Once again, state law must be consulted to determine whether a patient's authorization or a court order is required before disclosures are made in these circumstances. If these are not required by state law, a healthcare provider may disclose information about a patient to law enforcement under the Privacy Rule, if law enforcement asks for assistance by contacting the facility directly or seeks assistance in the news media to locate a suspect, fugitive, material witness, or missing person.

The decision to assist law enforcement in this situation is entirely up to the healthcare provider. It is helpful to establish criteria so the decision to report is consistent; criteria may include: the effect on the patient, the severity of the reported crime, the danger to society if this person is not caught, the perception of the public, and the healthcare mission versus the need to be a responsible member of the community.

Finally, if the decision to report is made and the information is not otherwise restricted by law, there is only very limited information that can be disclosed. This can include date and time of treatment. Because the purpose of the disclosure is to assist law enforcement in locating the individual, it can be assumed that the permitted disclosure includes the fact the patient is about to be discharged.

References

Department of Health and Human Services. 45 CFR §§164.512(a); 164.512(f)(2); Department of Health and Human Services. 42CFR §§2.21, 2.63–67. Pritts, J. 2006. Who's on First: The Interplay of HIPAA's "Required by Law" Exception and State Law. *Journal of American Health Information Management Association* 77(8):68, 69, 74.

Scenario 28

What if I am called to serve on a jury, and I know the patient?

Alcohol and substance abuse laws

Federal Drug and Alcohol Treatment Program Regulations do not address this situation specifically. A patient who is receiving Program services cannot be identified without the patient's specific authorization. The best procedure is to ask to speak to the judge privately and state that you work for a Program covered by 42 CFR Part 2, and as such, you might know the patient. Call your legal counsel if the judge wants to know more information.

The HIPAA Privacy Rule does not specifically address this situation. If you are selected for jury duty and you know one of the parties involved because he or she has been a patient in your facility, you have an obligation as a potential juror to disclose that you know the party. However, there is no provision under the Privacy Rule that permits you to disclose that the party has been a patient of your facility.

The best option is to ask to speak to the judge in private. The judge should take both lawyers and the court reporter and meet with you in the judge's chambers. You can state that you are aware of the party through your employment, and as a healthcare provider employs you, that the knowledge you have of the party is protected by the HIPAA Privacy Rule. That should be sufficient for the judge to make a decision, but if necessary, the judge can order you to disclose more information; the Privacy Rule permits a disclosure in response to a court order. You will probably be excused from serving on the jury.

References

Department of Health and Human Services. 45 CFR §§164.502 (a), 164.512(e)(1); Department of Health and Human Services. 42 CFR §§2.21, 2.63–67

Scenario 29

Can we disclose blood alcohol results
when a driver has an accident?

 State and federal laws

KEY WORDS TO SEARCH: law enforcement notification, required reporting to law enforcement, impaired drivers, and motor vehicle accidents

It is important to analyze state laws to determine if there are any requirements for healthcare providers to report to law enforcement when they treat a patient who has a motor vehicle accident. If the state law requires a healthcare provider to provide blood alcohol or other tests, which demonstrate the impairment of a driver in a motor vehicle accident, then the HIPAA Privacy Rule permits such a disclosure. However, the healthcare provider must only disclose the information the state law says to report, even though the Privacy Rule may allow more information to be given to law enforcement.

Some states have laws regarding legal blood draws based on law enforcement orders. These laws may allow the law enforcement official to order the test if the patient is unconscious or to obtain a court order for that purpose. When the healthcare provider is ordered to draw the blood in these circumstances and test it, the specimen and the test results are considered legal evidence, and the specimen and results are ordered by statute or court to be given to the law enforcement officer.

When the patient, under state law, must consent to the test or refuses the test, an authorization from the patient should be sought to disclose the results. Also, if such a test is performed as part of the treatment of the patient, then an authorization, court order, subpoena, or other legal process valid under state law must be provided by law enforcement in order to provide the test results.

References

Department of Health and Human Services. 45 CFR §§164.512(a), 164.512(f)(1).

Scenario 30

Do we need authorizations or court orders to disclose information for child abuse investigations?

State and federal laws

KEY WORDS TO SEARCH: child abuse, child neglect, exploitation of a minor, required reporting by healthcare providers, and subpoena

Alcohol and substance abuse laws

Federal Drug and Alcohol Treatment Program Regulations allow the reporting of child abuse in response to state reporting requirements. However, an authorization from the patient or a court order is required to produce additional Program records for investigations.

The HIPAA Privacy Rule permits healthcare providers to report child abuse or neglect to appropriate government authorities. Often, state law also requires these reports.

When it comes to providing information to government officials or to law enforcement for the follow-up investigation of a report of child abuse, however, state laws need to be carefully analyzed. Look for state law wording that requires healthcare providers to produce evidence or records for child abuse investigations or for directives that cooperation or evidence must be produced by healthcare providers. If the disclosure is required by state law, the Privacy Rule will permit relevant information be given to law enforcement or to the government agency involved in the investigation.

If state law does not require records or other evidence be produced for these investigations, however, then the government agency or law enforcement must provide other valid authority. Such authority can be an authorization signed by a parent. If the parent is suspected of the abuse, a valid legal process, such as a court order, may be the only option under state law. If the government agency has subpoena powers, and the subpoena meets the requirements of the Privacy Rule, a subpoena may be the appropriate authority to produce records. Finally, if the government agency has assumed protective custody of the child, a representative of the agency with legal authority to act on behalf of the child may sign the authorization for the production of the records.

References

Department of Health and Human Services. 45 CFR §§164.512(a), 164.512(b)(1)(ii), 164.512(f)(1); 42CFR §2.16(c)(6).

Scenario 31

Does HIPAA apply to healthcare documentation generated by U.S. physicians if the care is provided outside the U.S.?

 International laws

Check the laws that apply to disclosure of medical information in the country where the healthcare is provided. Some European countries have laws against personal information being transmitted outside their country and require certain protections if information about their citizens is stored in another country. There may also be some restrictions in United States law about receiving individually identifiable personal information because of trade restrictions or national security concerns. Check the U.S. State Department's Web site for information related to possible restrictions.

The HIPAA Privacy Rule applies to the states and territories of the United States and is not international law. However, if a healthcare provider meets the definition of a covered entity and maintains the healthcare records of patients within the U.S., then the Privacy Rule provisions would apply, no matter where the healthcare is actually provided.

Because the country in which the healthcare is provided may have more stringent privacy protections that govern how its citizens' records are disclosed and maintained, it may be prudent to meet those standards as well.

References

Department of Health and Human Services. 45 CFR §160.103.

Scenario 32

What health information can we give to a medical examiner?

State and federal laws

KEY WORDS TO SEARCH: medical examiner, coroner, suspicious death, and unattended death

Alcohol and substance abuse laws

Federal Drug and Alcohol Treatment Program Regulations permit the Program to disclose information to government officials when they are investigating the cause of death of a patient.

State law should be consulted as to the information that can be produced at the request of medical examiners or coroners. Usually, the extent of their authority is broad enough to allow them to receive any information they believe is relevant to a case. State law will also indicate if there is a particular document that should be produced in order to produce release of the records, such as a coroner's subpoena.

The HIPAA Privacy Rule allows a healthcare provider to disclose protected health information to a medical examiner or coroner, or a person assigned those duties. This can include information needed to identify a deceased person, determine a cause of death, or other duties the medical examiner or coroner has been assigned by law.

As a medical examiner or coroner is a public official, it is acceptable to assume he or she is only requesting the information needed for the purpose. If a coroner's subpoena is not provided, steps should be taken to verify the identity and authority of the medical examiner to receive the protected health information. To do so, the medical examiner or coroner should provide a written statement, on official letterhead, establishing identity and the authorizing state statute for the activity. If the medical examiner's office sends an individual to pick up the records needed, verify that person's identity through agency identification badges or other official credentials, and preferably, a letter on official letterhead from the medical examiner stating the authority. An oral confirmation from the medical examiner's office is also acceptable when a written statement is impractical in the circumstances.

In the situation in which the coroner is on the facility's staff or employed by the facility in which the protected health information is maintained, the coroner should still provide the required subpoena or statement of authority prior to being given access to the records. In this case, the individual is functioning in a different role as an employee or healthcare provider than he or she does as a coroner, and the disclosure is not for treatment, payment or healthcare operations of the covered entity.

References

Department of Health and Human Services. 45 CFR §§164.512(g), 164.514(2); Department of Health and Human Services. 42 CFR § 2.15(b)(1).

Scenario 33

How long do we wait for objections in cases of civil subpoenas?

State and federal laws

KEY WORDS TO SEARCH: rules of civil procedure, trial rule, production of documents, subpoena, and civil action

Alcohol and substance abuse laws

Federal Drug and Alcohol Treatment Program Regulations require a signed authorization from a patient be included with a subpoena or court order with certain findings in addition to the subpoena. It is recommended that the Program's legal counsel direct when and if records are disclosed in response to legal processes.

To be in compliance with the HIPAA Privacy Rule, the key information that a covered entity must have in order to disclose protected health information in a civil, judicial, or administrative proceeding is that a qualified protective order has been filed to protect the information, or that the covered entity has adequate assurances that the patient is notified of the request to produce his or her record. The patient must also have an opportunity to object to the production of his or her record.

Both federal and state judicial branches have rules they follow for activities involving the judicial system. These include rules of civil procedure and of evidence and how evidence, such as records, may be acquired through the use of subpoenas. Each court will have rules that will state how long the party receiving a subpoena has until they must produce the records. In many cases, 15 days is the time period allotted after service of the subpoena and notice to the patient to produce the record.

It is recommended that you wait until the last few days prior to the date of production to allow the patient or his or her legal counsel time to object, but still allow yourself sufficient time to produce the records by the date they are due.

References

Department of Health and Human Services. 45 CFR §164.512(e); Department of Health and Human Services. 42 CFR § 2.61(b).

Scenario 34

How do we know that patients who are involved in civil cases have been notified of subpoenas for their records?

 State and federal laws

KEY WORDS TO SEARCH: rules of civil procedure, trial rule, production of documents, subpoena, and civil action

 Alcohol and substance abuse laws

Federal Drug and Alcohol Treatment Program Regulations require a signed authorization from a patient be included with a subpoena or court order with certain findings in addition to the subpoena. It is recommended that the Program's legal counsel direct if and when records are disclosed.

The HIPAA Privacy Rule allows a covered entity to disclose protected health information in a civil judicial or administrative proceeding if certain criteria are met, and if the covered entity is not a party to the proceeding. The Privacy Rule requires that the covered entity has adequate assurances that the patient's privacy is protected, either by a qualified protective order or by giving the patient sufficient information and notice to prevent the disclosure.

Both federal and state judicial branches have rules they follow for activities involving the judicial system. These include rules of civil procedure and of evidence, and how evidence, such as records, may be acquired through the use of subpoenas. Each court will have rules that state how notice is provided to the opposing party. The facility's legal counsel should determine what is adequate evidence of notice to the patient, and if the facility itself should provide the notice to the patient.

Civil subpoenas require that the opposing counsel is notified, and proof can consist of a copy of the subpoena and a notice of service or mailing by the issuer of the subpoena. The subpoena should state whether the patient is the plaintiff or the defendant, the records that have been subpoenaed, and the time for the patient to raise objections. This time should have elapsed and no objections filed, or when an objection has been filed, it should indicate that there has been resolution of the objection. Otherwise, the subpoena should allow sufficient time for the patient to object and give the patient information on how an objection can be filed. After a certain point in the legal process, a party to the case cannot communicate directly with the other party, only the party's attorney. However, notice to the patient's attorney is considered the same as notice to the patient.

When the patient is not a plaintiff or a defendant in the case, the notice can still be made the same way. When the patient cannot be located, the issuer of the subpoena needs to provide adequate details and certification of the attempts made to locate the patient. The alternative is to seek a qualified protective order.

References

Department of Health and Human Services. 45 CFR §164.512(e); Department of Health and Human Services. 42 CFR § 2.61(b); Department of Health and Human Services, Office for Civil Rights. Your Frequently Asked Questions On Privacy. 707, 708. Available online from http://www.dhhs.gov/ocr/hipaa/.

Scenario 35

Can search warrants be used to produce protected health information?

State and federal laws

KEY WORDS TO SEARCH: rules of criminal procedure, trial rule, production of documents, search warrant, criminal action

Alcohol and substance abuse laws

Federal Drug and Alcohol Treatment Program Regulations require a signed authorization from a patient or court order with certain findings in order to produce records. A search warrant will probably not meet these requirements, even though it is a court order. Records seized in this fashion may not be admissible in court. It is recommended that the Program's legal counsel be contacted immediately to address the issue with law enforcement or the prosecuting attorney involved in the case.

The HIPAA Privacy Rule allows a covered entity to disclose protected health information when served with a court order or a court ordered warrant. The Privacy Rule permits the disclosure, but the warrant may force the disclosure or the covered entity may face legal consequences if it does not comply.

As long as the warrant is produced from a court that has jurisdiction over the covered entity, the warrant is sufficient authority for the covered entity to produce records. The covered entity should be sure to review the warrant carefully and produce only the records described in the warrant.

References

Department of Health and Human Services. 45 CFR §164.512(f)(1); Department of Health and Human Services. 42 CFR § 2.61(b); 2003. *Confidentiality and Communication: A Guide to the Federal Drug and Alcohol Confidentiality Law and HIPAA*. Legal Action Center of the City of New York. 62.

Scenario 36

Are out-of-state subpoenas valid?

 State and federal laws

KEY WORDS TO SEARCH: production of documents, subpoena, administrative summons, and discovery request

The covered entity should consult with its legal counsel when served with an out of state subpoena. However, in general, a subpoena gets its authority from a court. The court needs to have jurisdiction over the state in which the covered entity does business and has its records. A state court has jurisdiction in its own state; a nonstate court does not. A federal district court has jurisdiction over certain states and not others. A circuit court of appeals has jurisdiction over certain regions of the country.

An attorney from out of state jurisdiction can obtain authority for a subpoena, however, by a process called, "localizing" in which the attorney can go through a local court. A local court's stamp can be seen on the subpoena in that case, and the subpoena becomes valid in the local jurisdiction.

A military court has jurisdiction over records of individuals in the military.

A federal court has jurisdiction anywhere in the United States for a federal criminal proceeding.

Usually, state administrative subpoenas are not valid outside state lines.

Prison inmate records are subject to special rules; contact legal counsel to clarify these situations.

Federal law enforcement or health oversight agencies have subpoena powers that are valid in the states and territories of the United States.

In order to be considered a "lawful" process in the HIPAA Privacy Rule, the subpoena needs to be issued through the authority of a court with jurisdiction. The covered entity may only disclose protected health information in response to a lawful process that meets the requirements of the Privacy Rule.

References

Department of Health and Human Services. 45 CFR §164.512(e)

Scenario 37

Can we report an impaired driver to law enforcement?

State and federal laws

KEY WORDS TO SEARCH: department of motor vehicles, driver's license, and impaired driver

Alcohol and substance abuse laws

Federal Drug and Alcohol Treatment Program Regulations do not permit the Program to disclose information to government officials without authorization, unless the report can be made without identifying the patient as receiving Program services, and the patient is an imminent danger to himself or others.

If the extent of impairment is such that this individual is an imminent risk to himself, herself, or others, and the individual is planning to drive anyway, there is a provision in the HIPAA Privacy Rule that allows for a healthcare provider to warn someone who can take action in the situation. This might mean a relative of the patient, or it might mean law enforcement.

However, if the impairment is not immediate but is more long term, such as a mental, emotional, or non-stable physical disability or disease that may impair the person's ability to exercise reasonable and ordinary control over a motor vehicle, the risk to that person and the public may be reduced by treatment. State laws or regulations need to be consulted. Some states have required reporting of impaired drivers to the state's drivers' license division, some have permitted reporting, and some have no reporting requirement at all.

If the state has required reporting of these conditions, the healthcare provider may report the condition as the Privacy Rule allows reporting, as required by law. Permissive reporting, however, which can be recognized in laws by such statements as "may report" or "immunity from any damages claimed as a result" is different. For states with permissive reporting or that are silent on the issue, unless there is an immediate threat by the impairment, there is no clear permission to report these cases in the Privacy Rule. An authorization should be obtained from the patient to report in these cases.

References

Department of Health and Human Services. 45 CFR §§164.512(a), 164.512(j); Department of Health and Human Services. 42 CFR § 2.13.

Scenario 38

Are we permitted to report impaired pilots to the FAA?

State and federal laws

KEY WORDS TO SEARCH: duty to warn

Alcohol and substance abuse laws

Federal Drug and Alcohol Treatment Program Regulations do not permit the Program to disclose information to government officials without authorization, unless the report can be made without identifying the patient as receiving Program services and the patient is an imminent danger to himself or others.

If the extent of a physical or mental impairment is such that this individual is an imminent risk to himself, herself, or others, and the individual is planning to fly anyway, there is a provision in the HIPAA Privacy Rule to allow for a healthcare provider to warn someone who can take action in the situation. This would probably mean the Federal Aviation Administration (FAA), or possibly even the pilot's employer.

If the healthcare provider determines a pilot has a disability or disease that may impair the pilot's ability to pilot a plane, but the provider does not know whether the pilot is going to fly again, it does not mean that a healthcare provider has an obligation to report the pilot to the FAA. The healthcare provider only has an obligation to inform the pilot about the seriousness of the condition. Without an obligation to report in law or regulation and absent a determination that the pilot is an immediate threat, the healthcare provider is not permitted to report a pilot to the FAA or to the pilot's employer unless the pilot signs an authorization for the disclosure. A pilot has an obligation to self-report to the FAA if he or she wants to continue to fly a plane. Sometimes, the pilot never plans to fly again, so he or she does not report to the FAA.

Unless there is an immediate threat by the impairment, there is no clear permission to report these cases in the Privacy Rule. An authorization needs to be obtained from the pilot before any reporting to the FAA or to his or her employer would be permitted.

References

Department of Health and Human Services. 45 CFR §§164.512(a), 164.512(j); Department of Health and Human Services. 42 CFR § 2.13.

Scenario 39

Are grand jury subpoenas sufficient to produce protected health information?

 State and federal laws

KEY WORDS TO SEARCH: production of documents, and grand jury

 Alcohol and substance abuse laws

Federal Drug and Alcohol Treatment Program Regulations require a signed authorization from a patient be included with a subpoena or court order with certain findings in addition to the subpoena. It is recommended that the Program's legal counsel direct if and when records are disclosed.

The HIPAA Privacy Rule treats a grand jury subpoena similarly to a court order. In some cases, a judge may manage the grand jury. The judge may issue orders for the production of records, as well as penalize parties for failure to produce the records. Or, a prosecuting attorney may issue a subpoena in the name of the grand jury. Because of the complexity of this question, it is important to obtain legal counsel before complying or failing to comply with one of these subpoenas.

If the subpoena is appropriate, the healthcare provider should limit the disclosure of records to what is required in the subpoena.

References

Department of Health and Human Services. 45 CFR §164.512(f)

Scenario 40

Can we report a patient who brings drug paraphernalia or other illegal substances into our facility?

State and federal laws

KEY WORDS TO SEARCH: drug paraphernalia, controlled substances

Alcohol and substance abuse laws

Federal Drug and Alcohol Treatment Program Regulations do permit Programs to disclose information to law enforcement without authorization when the patient has committed a crime on the premises. This information is restricted to the identity of the patient, information directly related to the crime, status as a patient, address and last known whereabouts. The report could also be made without identifying the patient as receiving Program services.

Drug paraphernalia and unknown substances can be considered contraband, and authorities, such as the Drug Enforcement Agency (DEA), recommend that such substances be turned over to local law enforcement. Disposal of contraband by the covered entity is not recommended.

The decision by the healthcare provider to report the identity of the patient who was in possession of these items should be governed by state law. If there is a state law requiring the identity of the person be reported, the HIPAA Privacy Rule permits this disclosure, as long as it is limited to what the reporting law requires. In no case should the healthcare provider disclose more than what the Privacy Rule allows.

If state law is permissive or silent on healthcare provider reporting, the healthcare provider must make a decision to report based on professional judgment and ethics. If the provider decides to report, the Privacy Rule permits it if the provider considered this a crime on the covered entity's premises. Possession of these items is usually considered a crime, and it could be considered a crime on the premises to bring them into the facility.

References

Department of Health and Human Services. 45 CFR §§164.512(a), 164.512(f)(5); Department of Health and Human Services. 42 CFR § 2.12(c)(5), Conversation, Drug Enforcement Agency, Oct 2006.

Scenario 41

Can we provide copies of records for a physician who has been called to testify in an assault case?

State and federal laws

KEY WORDS TO SEARCH: court rules, production of records or documents, and witness

Alcohol and substance abuse laws

Federal Drug and Alcohol Treatment Program Regulations do not permit the Program to disclose information in criminal investigations or prosecutions of a patient without a court making certain findings and issuing an order stating those findings. Only information as specified in the court order can be produced. An authorization from a victim could be obtained to disclose records, but records produced in response to an authorization may have limitations on how they can be used by law enforcement. Contact facility legal counsel before either the physician testifies or records are produced to verify that these requirements have been met.

Physicians would be permitted to review the records of the care they provided prior to their testimony under the healthcare operations provisions of the HIPAA Privacy Rule. Copies of records could be provided for their use, and they would be free to bring them along when appearing in court. It is possible that the judge could order these copies of the records to be turned over while in court.

However, there are appropriate rules of evidence that apply in criminal cases, and the appropriate process must be followed in order for the records to be considered evidence. Usually, in order to be considered evidence, records must be produced by the facility in response to a valid subpoena or court order.

References

Department of Health and Human Services. 45 CFR §§164.506(c)(4), 164.512; Department of Health and Human Services. 42 CFR §§ 2.23, 2.63.

Scenario 42

What are "administrative requests," and how do I know if they have authority for me to produce records?

State and federal laws

KEY WORDS TO SEARCH: administrative request, summons, investigative demand, subpoena, request for records, fraud, investigation, and warrant

Alcohol and substance abuse laws

Federal Drug and Alcohol Treatment Program Regulations require a signed authorization from a patient be included with a subpoena, or court order with certain findings in addition to the subpoena. It is recommended that the Program's legal counsel direct if and when records are disclosed.

Different types of legal processes are used by different agencies to request the production of records. These documents are called different names by different agencies. The Internal Revenue Service, for example, may issue a summons; a state Adult Protective Service may issue an administrative subpoena. These are often used in criminal prosecutions or investigations.

The first step is to determine whether the agency issuing these "administrative requests" has the authority to issue them. Most federal agencies provide the statutory or regulatory reference along with the "request" or provide the reference when asked for the information. Other agencies should be asked to provide a copy of their statutory or regulatory authority. The relevant statute or regulation should make it clear who has the authority to issue these, when they apply, and what information would be relevant for the purpose.

The HIPAA Privacy Rule states that these "requests" must meet certain requirements before the covered entity can produce the records. These requirements are: the information sought is relevant and material to a legitimate law enforcement inquiry, the request is reasonably specific and limited in scope for the purpose, and de-identified information is not an option. This three-part test is actually a restatement of laws that govern the issuance of any subpoena. However, even though the law enforcement agency may know these three determinations have been made prior to the issuance of the "request," the Privacy Rule implies that it is the responsibility of the covered entity to determine whether the three-part test has been met. Legal counsel should be sought to determine if the covered entity will accept that this is a basic requirement of the issuance of the "request" by an agency authorized to issue it, or if the law enforcement agency will be required to provide these specific statements in the "request" or in an attached document.

References

Department of Health and Human Services. 45 CFR §164.512(f)(1); Department of Health and Human Services. 42 CFR § 2.61(b).

Scenario 43

Are court-ordered medical evaluations regulated under HIPAA?

 State and federal laws

Key words to search: court rules, involuntary commitment, and competency hearing

If the healthcare provider who does a court-ordered medical evaluation is a covered entity, the medical evaluation will be considered an activity that creates information about the current physical or mental health of an individual. However, if the findings of a court-ordered medical evaluation are not used by the covered entity to make decisions about the individual, it can be argued that this information is not considered part of a designated record set. So, the protections of the HIPAA Privacy Rule apply, but not necessarily the rights of the individual in regards to these records, unless they are being used by the covered entity to make decisions about the patient.

If a covered entity receives the medical evaluation results in order to care for the individual as the result of a commitment hearing, for example, the evaluation may be used to make treatment decisions about a patient, and it would, therefore, become part of the individual's designated record set.

The court orders these evaluations and will direct the healthcare provider to disclose the results to the court or to other involved parties. A court-ordered disclosure is permitted in the Privacy Rule.

References

Department of Health and Human Services. 45 CFR §§160.103, 164.501, 164.512(e).

Scenario 44

If a patient has committed a crime, can healthcare providers warn other providers in the area about the patient?

State and federal laws

KEY WORDS TO SEARCH: duty to warn, Tarasoff

Alcohol and substance abuse laws

Federal Drug and Alcohol Treatment Program Regulations do not permit the Program to disclose information to other treatment providers without authorization, except in emergency treatment situations.

There are situations in which patients commit crimes against healthcare providers, such as when a patient steals a prescription pad or forges the provider's name. Often, a healthcare provider feels the need to warn his or her peers about the patient's activities. However, the HIPAA Privacy Rule allows covered entities to only disclose the information about a crime against them to a law enforcement official. The appropriate action in this case is to report the crime to law enforcement and allow law enforcement to warn other healthcare providers in the area, if they feel the warning is justified.

If the patient is threatening to harm other specific healthcare providers, and the provider who hears the threat is convinced there is an imminent risk of harm to these providers, there is a provision in the Privacy Rule to allow for a healthcare provider to warn other persons. If these providers are the targets of the threats, the healthcare provider can warn the other specific healthcare providers who are being threatened. However, be sure to check state laws to see if this disclosure is limited to law enforcement.

References

Department of Health and Human Services. 45 CFR §§164.502(l)(2), 164.512(j); Department of Health and Human Services. 42 CFR § 2.13.

Scenario 45

Can we disclose a patient's name if he or she has a communicable disease?

 State and federal laws

KEY WORDS TO SEARCH: communicable disease, bioterrorism, and exposure

 Alcohol and substance abuse laws
Federal Drug and Alcohol Treatment Program Regulations do not permit this disclosure when it identifies the patient as part of the Program. The disclosure must either be made with a signed authorization by the patient, or without identifying the patient as being part of the Program.

Most states require reporting of communicable diseases as part of the need to protect public health. In the case of public health reporting, a covered entity may disclose this information under the HIPAA Privacy Rule under one of two sections: first, there is a specific provision in the Privacy Rule that permits covered entities to disclose information as required by other laws; or second, thee Privacy Rule allows the disclosure of information for the purpose of public health, disease prevention, or control. It should be noted, too, that even if a state public health law appears to give a patient less privacy than what is required by the Privacy Rule, it still must be followed. The Privacy Rule exempts state public health statutes from being pre-empted by HIPAA.

Within the covered entity itself, Medicare conditions of participation and state licensure rules generally require that the covered entity has an infection control plan. Part of the plan is the need to identify sources of infection, as well as to identify individuals who may be exposed to a communicable disease. An infection control nurse should have the right to use and disclose protected health information related to the communicable disease under the healthcare operations provisions of the Privacy Rule, since such activities are critical to the business of healthcare, and the access is appropriate for the employee's assigned role in the organization. However, because healthcare operations are subject to the minimum necessary provisions of the Privacy Rule, the infection control nurse should only access and share information needed for the investigation, and only to other employees who need to know the information. For example, it may be necessary for a nursing supervisor over an affected department to be told the identity of the individual who has the communicable disease, in order to determine which patients or employees have been exposed; but an entire department probably does not need to know the identity of the individual, just that an exposure occurred.

Finally, if an individual is found to have a highly contagious disease, it is best to involve the public health agency to notify others who may be exposed. Even when state laws do not specifically require such disclosures, the duty to warn provision in the Privacy

Rule allows disclosures to be made by the covered entity to prevent or lessen a serious and imminent threat to the health of a person or the public. These disclosures can be made to someone who can lessen the threat, such as the health department, or to the person who is in danger.

References

Department of Health and Human Services. 45 CFR §§ 160.203(c), 164.512(a), (b) and(j); Department of Health and Human Services. 42 CFR § 2.12.

Scenario 46

Am I allowed to release information to law enforcement in a domestic abuse case?

 State and federal laws

KEY WORDS TO SEARCH: law enforcement notification, required reporting of victims of crimes, investigations, subpoena, warrant, court order, duty to warn, and Tarasoff

 Alcohol and substance abuse laws

Federal Drug and Alcohol Treatment Program Regulations require a patient's signed authorization to allow disclosure of records to law enforcement, unless there is a court order that permits such disclosures.

There are two potential disclosures made in the situation of domestic abuse. The first is the reporting of the abuse, and second is the disclosure of records to law enforcement when they come to investigate the crime and gather evidence.It is important to analyze state laws to determine what circumstances require healthcare providers to report domestic violence to law enforcement.

If the state law requires a healthcare provider to notify law enforcement in these situations, then the HIPAA Privacy Rule permits such a disclosure. The Privacy Rule allows the disclosure to be made to law enforcement, a social service, or protective services agency that is authorized by law to receive these reports. However, the victim needs to agree to the disclosure, either verbally, with documentation by the healthcare provider, or in writing. If the victim does not agree, then healthcare providers may still report the incident if they decide that the disclosure is necessary to prevent serious harm to either the victim or to others. The victim must be informed about the disclosure unless it would increase the danger. This means that when informing a patient's personal representative, the healthcare provider can also be silent about the disclosure if informing the victim's personal representative means informing the very person who may be responsible for the abuse.

If victims cannot agree to the disclosure because they are incapacitated, the healthcare provider may still report if the law enforcement or other agency states that immediate action is needed to apprehend the person responsible for the abuse and that the information will not be used against the victim. This certification should probably be in writing.

If the state law is silent on such reporting, or permits but does not require reporting of domestic abuse, then the report may be made either with the authorization of the victim or when the healthcare provider decides the threat of future violence to this individual or others is serious and imminent. They may report under the "Duty to Warn" provision of the Privacy Rule.

When law enforcement or other agencies request records for a follow up investigation, state laws should be consulted as well. Most of the time, there is not a statutory provision that requires a healthcare provider to turn over records for investigations. The investigators should provide a HIPAA complaint authorization signed by the victim or provide a subpoena or court order. The validity of subpoenas or other legal process documents is also dependent on state laws and court rules, so the covered entity's legal counsel should be consulted to make the determination of validity.

References

Department of Health and Human Services. 45 CFR §§164.512(a), (c), (j).

SECTION IV

Employee Records and HIPAA

This section reviews scenarios that relate to records created for employment purposes in which a healthcare provider is also the individual's employer. It analyzes when HIPAA applies to employee records and when it does not.

Scenario 47

Are occupational health records regulated under HIPAA?

 State and federal labor and worker's compensation laws

KEY WORDS TO SEARCH: labor, Labor Commission, workplace testing, workplace safety, workplace illness or injury, Department of Transportation or Federal Aviation Administration (FAA), Occupational Safety and Health Administration (OSHA), and Mine Safety and Health Administration (MSHA)

As long as the healthcare provider who is providing the occupational health services is a covered entity under the HIPAA Privacy Rule, the individually identifiable records generated for occupational health purposes are covered under the Privacy Rule.

Covered entities that provide these types of services are required to give a notice to the individual that if treatment relates to medical surveillance of the workplace or to a work-related illness or injury, the information will be disclosed to his or her employer. Frequently, the healthcare provider will ask the individual to sign a conditional authorization in order to provide the employer with copies of preplacement physicals, drug tests, and fitness-for-duty examinations. The employer usually pays for these, and they are a condition of employment, so the individual can be denied the service if he or she does not sign the conditional authorization. These types of authorization are valid under the Privacy Rule.

However, the healthcare provider, who is providing only occupational health services, may not be a covered entity under the HIPAA Privacy Rule. This is not an unusual situation, as payment for this type of service is done by contract with employers. Although they are healthcare providers, they do not meet the second requirement of being a covered entity: the covered entity must transmit health information in electronic form in connection with a covered transaction. In this case, the records would not be subject to the provisions of the Privacy Rule.

References

Department of Health and Human Services, 45 CFR §§160.103, 164.512(b), 164.508(b)(4)(iii) ; Department of Health and Human Services, Office for Civil Rights. Your Frequently Asked Questions On Privacy. 301. Available online from http://www.dhhs.gov/ocr/hipaa/.

Scenario 48

When the healthcare facility is self-insured for employee health insurance, what information can be shared with human resources?

State and federal labor and worker's compensation laws

KEY WORDS TO SEARCH: Americans with Disabilities Act (ADA), state employment laws, and ERISA

Alcohol and substance abuse laws

Federal Drug and Alcohol Treatment Program Regulations require that a consent or authorization be obtained from the patient to disclose information for payment purposes. Unless the consent or authorization specifically permits redisclosure to the employer, the information cannot be redisclosed to the employer.

When a healthcare facility is self-insured, it is considered an employer and the sponsor of a health plan.

Some healthcare systems are also health plans. Obviously, healthcare facilities are also healthcare providers. The best way to determine the appropriate application of the Privacy Rule in this very confusing structure is to consider the covered entity as separate "companies" with different functions.

The activities of the employer "company" human resources department, or whoever administers the plan on behalf of the employees, are technically not regulated under the Privacy Rule. However, the Privacy Rule extends its protections to the use of the protected health information (PHI) by the plan sponsor (the employer "company") through the use of plan documents to restrict the use and disclosure of the information.

As a health plan "company," the disclosure of information to the plan sponsor (employer "company") is permitted when it is summary data. If it is individually identifiable, then the health plan "company" must have certification from the plan sponsor (employer "company") that they have the required plan documents. In a plan document, the employer "company" agrees to: (1) not use or disclose the PHI other than as permitted or required in the plan documents or by law; (2) ensure that any of its subcontractors or agents agree to the same restrictions; (3) not use or disclose PHI for employment-related actions; (4) report back to the health plan any disclosures that were not permitted by law or the plan document; (5) make the PHI accessible to individuals; (6) allow the individuals to request amendments; (7) provide an accounting of disclosures; (8) allow the Secretary of Health and Human Services access to determine compliance; (9) return and destroy all PHI when no longer needed; and (10) ensure there are adequate separations between health plan records and plan sponsor (employer "company") records, such as a firewall. Finally, the plan must restrict access to the PHI supplied by the health plan "company" to certain employees, often human resources employees, and only for those employees to conduct plan-related business.

References

Department of Health and Human Services. 45 CFR § 164.504 (f–g); Department of Health and Human Services. 42 CFR § 2.12(c)(3). Department of Health and Human Services. 2000. Final Rule: Standards for the Privacy of Individually Identifiable Health Information. *Federal Register* 65(250):82509.

Scenario 49

Can employee medical records be used in infection control investigations?

State and federal labor and worker's compensation laws

Occupational Safety and Health Administration (OSHA) regulations, Medicare Conditions of Participation

> **KEY WORDS TO SEARCH:** communicable disease, Medicare Conditions of
> Participation

Alcohol and substance abuse laws

Federal Drug and Alcohol Treatment Program Regulations may cover Employee Assistance Program (EAP) records. These regulations do allow access to records by the entity having direct administrative control over the Program in order to continue to provide services; therefore, if access to these records by an infection control nurse was considered necessary to maintain the Program, it would be permitted.

Employee health records are specifically excluded from being covered in the HIPAA Privacy Rule. Other state and federal regulations, such as OSHA, apply to these records. These regulations should be consulted before disclosure is made to the infection control investigator.

However, a healthcare employee may have general medical records created by the covered entity if the employee has also been a patient of the covered entity. The healthcare provider has an obligation by state law, Medicare Conditions of Participation, and accreditation requirements to have an infection control plan. Part of this plan includes the investigation of sources of infection and steps to prevent further infection. If the infection information is only found in the employee's general medical record, the information can be accessed as part of an infection control investigation by an infection control nurse, being that this activity can be considered either a part of the treatment activities of the healthcare provider (management of health care and related services) or healthcare operations (quality improvement) in the HIPAA Privacy Rule and is, therefore, a permitted use of protected health information.

Therefore, review of an employee's protected health information by the facility infection control investigator is permitted if the employee is believed to be infected with a communicable disease or to have been exposed to a communicable disease, but the access should be restricted to the information necessary for the infections disease investigation.

References

Department of Health and Human Services. 45 CFR §§ 160.103 (2), (iii), 164.501; Department of Health and Human Services. 42 CFR § 2.12(c)(3).

Scenario 50

Can employees obtain copies of their pre-employment physicals or employee drug tests under HIPAA?

 State and federal labor and worker's compensation laws

KEY WORDS TO SEARCH: labor, labor commission, workplace testing, workplace safety, workplace illness or injury, Department of Transportation, Federal Aviation Administration, Occupational Safety and Health Administration (OSHA), or Mine Safety and Health Administration (MSHA)

An individual may obtain results of a physical examination or a drug test if these tests are provided by a covered entity in its capacity as a covered entity. For example, if the worker goes to a healthcare provider who is providing the occupational health services and the healthcare provider is a covered entity under the HIPAA Privacy Rule, the individually identifiable records generated for occupational health purposes are under the Privacy Rule. In that case, if the healthcare provider retains the records, the Privacy Rule provisions apply, and, therefore, the individual can access his or her records. If the occupational health provider is not a covered entity under the Privacy Rule, workers may or may not be able to obtain their test results, unless other state or federal laws grant them such access.

If the same test results are maintained in the clinical records of a covered entity as well as an employment record, the Privacy Rule applies to the first information, but not the second. Immunization records may reside in both records, but a treating physician uses the immunization records in making treatment decisions about the individual, whereas the employer may use the same information to determine if the employe is protected from transmitting communicable diseases in the workplace, as required by state licensure laws.

Once the test results are disclosed to the worker's employer by authorization, the test results become part of the employee's employment record. These test results, after being filed in an employee's employment record, are no longer protected health information, and other laws and regulations apply to them. In many cases, a worker may be able to obtain copies of the results, but the authority for the access is not the Privacy Rule, it is another law or regulation.

References

Department of Health and Human Services. 45 CFR §§160.103, 164.524; Department of Health and Human Services. Final Modifications to the Privacy Rule, August 2002. *Federal Register* 67(157):53193–4

Scenario 51

Are Employee Assistance Programs or Employee Ask-A-Nurse Programs subject to HIPAA?

Alcohol and substance abuse laws

An Employee Assistance Program (EAP), to the extent that it refers or treats individuals for drug or alcohol dependency, and whether it receives federal funding either directly or indirectly, may be a covered program and subject to the Federal Drug and Alcohol Treatment Program Regulations.

Some treatment activities are not necessarily subject to the HIPAA Privacy Rule. Employee Assistance Programs (EAP) and Ask-A-Nurse Programs do not engage in covered transactions; therefore, they may not meet the requirements of being a covered entity. Some EAPs do not provide treatment, either.

The covered healthcare organization that engages in these program activities has two choices. If the organization decides it does not want to apply the Privacy Rule to these activities, the organization must designate itself as a hybrid entity. The drawbacks with this approach are that the covered division of the hybrid entity must not disclose any information to the EAP or Ask-a-Nurse Program, except what is allowed in the Privacy Rule. Information for treatment or payment of the treatment of an individual may be shared, but the Privacy Rule covered providers can only share information on a very limited basis for healthcare operations. Any identifiable information must be kept electronically or physically separate. Finally, if a person performs duties for both the covered and noncovered divisions, the person may not use or disclose protected health information received when performing services for the covered entity to the noncovered program.

Alternatively, the healthcare organization may decide to include these programs as part of its covered entity, and, therefore, must apply the provisions of the Privacy Rule to the EAP or Ask-a-Nurse Programs. The drawback, of course, is that the Privacy Rule provisions must be applied in these settings, such as Notice of Privacy Practices provisions. However, this organization will permit more uses and disclosures of protected health information within the covered entity.

References

Department of Health and Human Services. 2000. Final Rule: Standards for the Privacy of Individually Identifiable Health Information. *Federal Register* 65(250):82576; Department of Health and Human Services. 45 CFR §§ 164.500, 164, 105, 164.506; 42 CFR § 2.12.

SECTION V

An Individual's Rights and Permission to Disclose

This section discusses a variety of scenarios that involve the rights established for individuals in HIPAA. Many of the scenarios address the complicated situation in determining personal representative status, when dealing with a deceased person's records, or parents to a child's records. Several scenarios discuss the disclosure of information to families, a situation that is often a concern to healthcare providers since HIPAA was enacted.

Scenario 52

Can we ever release psychotherapy notes to a patient?

State and federal laws

KEY WORDS TO SEARCH: consent, authorization, mental or behavioral health treatment, psychotherapy, mental health therapists, and duty to warn (Tarasoff)

Alcohol and substance abuse laws

Federal Drug and Alcohol Treatment Programs state that a Program is not prohibited from providing access of patients to their own records. If a Program is also a covered entity under the HIPAA Privacy Rule, there is no conflict between the regulations by applying the Privacy Rule provisions to any psychotherapy notes the Program maintains.

In order to be considered psychotherapy notes in the HIPAA Privacy Rule, notes must meet the following criteria: they must be created by a mental health professional, must document or analyze conversations occurring in a private, group, joint, or family counseling session, and must be maintained separately from the rest of the individual's medical record. The Privacy Rule also defines a list of documents that cannot be considered psychotherapy notes; this list includes documents normally found in an individual's mental health record.

The Privacy Rule restricts the use of psychotherapy notes, even within a covered entity, to certain treatment, payment, or healthcare operations. It only allows disclosures by law when the covered entity must defend itself in a legal action brought by the individual to the Secretary of Health and Human Services to determine compliance with the Privacy Rule, when required by law, for health oversight of the therapist; to a medical examiner in cases of death; and under duty to warn situations.

The Privacy Rule also states that an individual has no right to access this information, unlike nearly every other designated record set. A decision to deny access to this record cannot be appealed.

However, should the author of the psychotherapy notes decide to provide access to these records to the individual, this access is not prohibited either. The question then arises: If the author decides to provide this access, is there a requirement to obtain an authorization from the individual before the access can be granted? On one hand, nearly every other disclosure of psychotherapy notes requires that an authorization be signed. On the other hand, no requirement exists in the Privacy Rule that states that an individual must sign a HIPAA compliant authorization before obtaining access to records. It requires close reading, but there is a provision early in the section addressing psychotherapy notes that excempts the individual from an authorization requirement. Therefore, an authorization from individuals would not be required before access is provided to their psychotherapy notes, unless otherwise required by state law.

References

Department of Health and Human Services. 45 CFR §§164.501, 164.508, 164.524.

Scenario 53

Does an individual have the right to opt out of being listed in a facility directory, yet demand we provide information to specific people when they call?

The HIPAA Privacy Rule allows individuals to decide whether they wish to be listed in a facility directory when they are admitted to a facility. The directory information usually includes the patient's name, location in the facility, and the general condition of the patient. If the patient decides to be listed in the facility directory, the patient should be informed that only callers who know his or her name will be be given any of this limited information. Religious affiliation is also often listed with the patient's permission, in case the patient would like a visit from clergy of the patient's denomination.

The covered entity must provide the individual with the choice to restrict or prohibit some or all of these uses or disclosures.

Most entities have interpreted this as giving an individual a choice to be listed in or not listed in the directory, nothing in between. "Out of the directory" means that all disclosures to visitors or callers are prohibited. Often this ban is absolute. No calls will be forwarded, and no flowers delivered. If patients want visitors to know where they are, the patients themselves or their family must inform visitors. The assumption is that these patients are requesting absolute privacy.

Covered entities generally do not provide screening of visitors or of calls for patients because such an activity is too difficult to manage. Too many employees and volunteers are involved in the process of forwarding calls and directing visitors for the covered entity to ensure that patients' requests are honored. If a covered entity agreed to this screening and could not meet the agreement, it could be considered a violation of this standard of the Privacy Rule.

The restriction or prohibition of some information is usually applied to the question of clergy. The restriction is easy enough to implement; the patient need only indicate that he or she does not want to list a denomination. As clergy visiting lists are only provided based on a patient's denomination, no external clergyperson would be provided the patient's name.

References

Department of Health and Human Services. 45 CFR §164.510.

Scenario 54

What kinds of information about a patient's condition can we disclose to callers?

 Alcohol and substance abuse laws
Federal Drug and Alcohol Treatment Programs require the patient to sign an authorization or a properly constituted order of a court prior to disclosure of information identifying the patient as receiving Program treatment services.

The HIPAA Privacy Rule allows patients to choose whether they wish to be included in a facility directory. If they choose to be included, visitors or callers who know the patient's name can be provided his or her location in the facility or room phone number, as well as the patient's "condition, which can only be described in general terms that do not communicate specific medical information about the individual . . ."

Therefore, the covered entity can choose a way of describing a patient's condition as long as it does not communicate specific medical information. Neither is it restricted to a one-word description of a condition, nor is it limited to certain adjectives. However, common practice is to use the conditions published by the American Hospital Association. They are:

♦ Undetermined: Patient is awaiting physician and/or assessment.

♦ Good: Vital signs are stable and within normal limits. Patient is conscious and comfortable. Indicators are excellent.

♦ Fair: Vital signs are stable and within normal limits. Patient is conscious, but may be uncomfortable. Indicators are favorable.

♦ Serious: Vital signs may be unstable and not within normal limits. Patient is acutely ill. Indicators are questionable.

♦ Critical: Vital signs are unstable and not within normal limits. Patient may be unconscious. Indicators are unfavorable.

It is permitted for the covered entity's employee disclosing the condition of the patient to read the definition of the condition to the visitor, if requested. The definition of the conditions used by the covered entity may be displayed on its public Web site or in other published documents. However, it is not permitted for the covered entity's employee to give the caller any further information other than the general condition of the patient who is listed in the facility directory. Additional requests for information should be referred to the patient, the patient's family, or the patient's healthcare provider to make a determination of the caller's involvement in the care of the patient.

References

Department of Health and Human Services. 45 CFR §164.510. American Hospital Association. 2003. HIPAA Updated Guidelines for Releasing Information on Conditions of Patients. Available online from www.aha.org/aha/advisory/2003/030201-media-adv. html/.

Scenario 55

Should employees be allowed to access their own protected health information electronically?

Allowing the employees of a covered entity to access their own protected health information electronically results in a situation in which the covered entity may be in compliance with parts of the HIPAA Privacy Rule, but in violation of other sections of the Privacy Rule.

Access by individuals to their protected health information, except in very limited situations, is a right established by the Privacy Rule. Minimum necessary does not apply to these disclosures. Even though there are maximum time limits to provide the protected health information, there is nothing that prevents the covered entity from providing immediate, on-line access. Finally, the covered entity should provide the access to the individual in a form or format requested by the individual, if it is readily producible in such a form. If an individual already has access to electronic records as a member of a covered entity, it makes it very easy for the covered entity to comply with that individual's desire for access. Therefore, allowing an employee access to his or her own information appears congruent with the intent of the Privacy Rule in regard to the individual's rights.

On the other hand, as members of the workforce, employees should only have access to information based on their job role and to information necessary to carry out their duties. Allowing employees to access their own records using their job-based access rights appears to violate these minimum necessary standards. Also, the covered entity may have decided that all requests for access must be in writing; therefore, employees accessing their own information would be in violation of that policy. Finally, allowing employees to use job-based access rights may endanger the integrity of the data, given that employees might have rights to change the information as well as review it.

An ideal situation may be to establish a patient portal through which all patients may view their own records in a secure manner, and for which an employee has no more or no less rights than any other patient.

Each covered entity must decide where it stands on this issue. If a covered entity has a long-established culture in which employees have been allowed access to their own records, it may be a major disruption of the covered entity to try to sanction large numbers of employees for reviewing their own records.

In support of not allowing the access, experience has shown that if employees make a practice of accessing their own records outside of job responsibilities, they tend to feel free to access the records of friends and family as well, which may be a violation of the Privacy Rule. Finally, allowing access to some employees because of existing job-based access rights, while not allowing other employees the same degree of access because their jobs do not require access to electronic systems, might lead to an appearance of discrimination.

References

Department of Health and Human Services. 45 CFR §§ 164.524, 164, 514.

Scenario 56

Can a parent with joint custody of a child living in a different state obtain copies of the child's mental health treatment records?

State and federal laws

KEY WORDS TO SEARCH: minor, parent, guardian, age of majority, consent to mental health treatment, and custody of minor children

Alcohol and substance abuse laws

Drug and Alcohol Treatment Program Federal Record Regulations require signing an authorization to allow disclosure of records to a parent.

Determining if a parent has access to his or her child's mental health treatment records requires extensive research into state law. First, determine whether there is a state law that specifies that a minor alone must consent for mental health treatment. If the parent consented for the treatment of the minor, it would imply that the parent should be allowed access to any records generated during the encounter.

Another item to check with the covered entity's legal counsel is whether a parent loses parental rights in a divorce. Often, when there are no abuse issues, both parents will retain the right to access their biological or adopted children's records, regardless of who has custody. This is only logical, because a parent may be directly involved in a child's care during a child's visits, or possibly even as the guarantor or primary insured on the policy that covers the child.

A parent from another state may have to prove his or her identity as the parent of the child and provide proof of relationship, under the verification requirements of the Privacy Rule.

On the other hand, many states allow nonemancipated minors of a certain age to consent to their own treatment in mental health therapy. In those states, the minor must authorize the disclosure before it can be made to the parent. State law would also need to be consulted to determine who could authorize the disclosure if the minor is incapable of doing so.

Also, the healthcare provider could deny the request if the provider believes there is a danger to the minor from the parent if such a disclosure was made, and could also check to see if there is a court order on file that revokes the parental rights of the parent requesting the records. The healthcare provider can choose not to treat the parent as a personal representative in that case.

References

Department of Health and Human Services. 45 CFR §§164.502(g) i–iii, 164.502(g) 5, 164.512(j); Department of Health and Human Services. 42 CFR § 2.14.

Scenario 57

Do parents have the right to access their children's records to see if they are sexually active?

State and federal laws

KEY WORDS TO SEARCH: minor, emancipated, pregnant, sexually transmitted disease, contraceptive services, parent, guardian, age of majority, consent to treatment, sexual assault, and abortion

Alcohol and substance abuse laws

Federal Drug and Alcohol Treatment Program Regulations require a minor's signed authorization to allow disclosure of records to a parent, unless the minor is incapable of understanding the request because of age or impairment.

In order to determine if a parent can access their children's records of sexual activity, state law must be reviewed. Some states do not specifically prohibit the disclosure of sexual activity of a minor to a parent. In these states, if the parent consented to the treatment of the minor for the clinical encounter, or for a physical examination of the minor, and sexual activity was documented as part of that examination, it would imply that the parent should be allowed access to any records generated during the encounter.

Alternatively, if state law mandates or permits the requested disclosure to the parent, it must be made. Some state laws require the parent to be informed of certain types of treatment related to the sexual activity of minors, such as when a minor is considering an abortion.

If the state law does not specifically address whether a minor is required to authorize to disclose his or her own treatment information, the healthcare provider must use professional judgment to make the decision whether to allow access by parents.

Finally, if there is a serious and imminent threat to the life or health of the minor because of sexual activity, the parent may be given access in order to deal with the dangerous behavior.

If there is a state law that specifically prohibits disclosure of the records of sexual activity of a minor to the parent, the minor must authorize the disclosure.

Some states allow nonemancipated minors to consent to their own treatment in certain circumstances. In those cases, the state law may also stipulate whether the minor must authorize the disclosure of related records. If the minor seeks treatment in these states, and if the state law specifies that he or she alone must authorize disclosure of related information, the minor must sign for the parent to have access.

Also, if the parent is involved in the sexual activity of the minor, the healthcare provider can choose not to treat the parent as a personal representative and deny the access based on that reason.

References

Department of Health and Human Services. 2000. Final Rule: Standards for the Privacy of Individually Identifiable Health Information. *Federal Register* 65(250); Department of Health and Human Services. 45 CFR §§164.502(g) i–iii, 164.502(g) 5, 164.512(j); Department of Health and Human Services. 42 CFR § 2.14.

Scenario 58

Does HIPAA prevent parents from being in the same room as their child when the child is receiving healthcare?

The HIPAA Privacy Rule does not restrict a parent from physically being in the room with a child receiving care. The Privacy Rule addresses the privacy rights of individuals to their protected health information and rules for the use and disclosure of that information. However, although the Rule does not address a parent being in the same room, it does require the parent be allowed access to a child's records as a personal representative, except in extraordinary circumstances. The only situation even remotely related to this question in the Privacy Rule is when an adult patient asks a provider not to share protected health information in front of a family member or friend.

A healthcare provider may restrict individuals from being in certain areas of the facility because of policy or safety concerns. These areas may be restricted because of hazardous equipment or substances or because of the need to keep the areas as sterile as possible for patient care, such as the case with operating rooms. Also, if the healthcare provider suspects possible abuse of the child, the provider may ask the parent not to be present during the interview and examination of the child. These situations have nothing to do with the Privacy Rule.

References

Department of Health and Human Services. 45 CFR §§164.502(g) i–iii, 164.512(b)(2), 164.524(a).

Scenario 59

Does HIPAA define what can be charged for record copies?

 State and federal laws

KEY WORDS TO SEARCH: copy costs for medical records

The HIPAA Privacy Rule only addresses fees for copying protected health information in one circumstance.

The intent of the Rule is to allow an individual to obtain copies of records for a fee that is reasonable enough that an individual could pay it. Therefore, the Privacy Rule only addresses what can be charged to individuals for copies of their own records.

The Privacy Rule requires that the copy fee for the individual be reasonable and cost based. It can only include the costs of labor for copying, supplies for copying, and postage, when mailed. It does not set a certain per-page amount. If the individual prefers a summary of his or her information, the fee to create that summary must be approved by the individual in advance.

The commentary to the Privacy Rule expands upon this standard. If paper copies of the records are made, the fee can include the cost of the paper. If electronic copies are made, the fee can include copies of the media used. The commentary also states that the covered entity may not charge a fee for record retrieval or handling.

The covered entity should determine the costs to individuals based on a study of the process. The commentary notes that even when state law establishes a charge, the covered entity cannot charge this amount unless it is equal to or less than the actual costs of copying and supplies. Therefore, it is important that the covered entity establish and document what these costs are, should the amount the covered entity charges be challenged.

The Privacy Rule also limits the fees to be charged to a personal representative. A personal representative is a person who has the authority to act for an adult or emancipated minor in making decisions related to the individual's healthcare. For a minor, it is the minor's parent, guardian, or other person acting *in loco parentis* who has authority to make decisions related to healthcare. For a deceased individual, a personal representative is the executor, administrator, or other person who has authority to act on behalf of a deceased individual or his or her estate.

Otherwise, the fee limitations in the Privacy Rule do not apply to other copying requests to the covered entity for treatment, payment, or healthcare operations, based on authorizations signed by the patient, or disclosures by law.

References

Department of Health and Human Services. 45 CFR §§ 164.502(g), 164.524(c)(4); Department of Health and Human Services. 2000. Final Rule: Standards for the Privacy of Individually Identifiable Health Information. *Federal Register* 65(250): 82558; Final Modifications to the Privacy Rule August. 2002. *Federal Register* 67(157): 53255.

Scenario 60

Who is the personal representative for a deceased person?

 State and federal laws

KEY WORDS TO SEARCH: executor, personal representative, probate, next of kin, and guardianship

The Privacy Rule considers the personal representative of a deceased individual as the executor, administrator, or other person who has authority to act on behalf of a deceased individual or the deceased individual's estate. It is important to consult state law regarding who can be considered a personal representative when a person dies.

In the absence of a state law and for cases in which there is no executor named for an estate, common practice is to allow the spouse of the individual to be considered the personal representative. Alternatively, when there is no spouse, an adult child of the deceased may be considered a personal representative. Professional judgment often applies in these cases. If a healthcare provider has been disclosing information to the spouse up until the patient dies, then it is reasonable to consider the spouse as the personal representative of the deceased person.

However, when there is a dispute as to who should be considered the personal representative of the deceased, the healthcare provider can ask for proof of executorship before providing copies of the information.

A question often comes up in cases in which a person has created a healthcare power of attorney, and this person seeks to be considered the personal representative after the patient is deceased. Technically, the healthcare power of attorney provides the right to make healthcare decisions about a patient when the patient is no longer able to make these decisions, but is no longer valid after the person dies. Should the patient wish this person to also be considered his or her personal representative after the patient's death, the patient should name this person as the executor of his or her estate.

References

Department of Health and Human Services. 45 CFR §§ 164.502(g), 164.524(c)(4).

Scenario 61

If we release records appropriately, but the records are misused, do we have to account for the disclosure?

The HIPAA Privacy Rule establishes that an individual be able to request an accounting of all disclosures of the individual's protected health information. There are exceptions: treatment, payment, and healthcare operations are excepted, disclosures to the individuals themselves, incidental disclosures that occur when the covered entity is appropriately disclosing information, disclosure from the facility directory or to persons involved in the care of the patient, or for notification purposes, and disclosures of limited data sets. Rarely used exceptions are disclosures made for national security or intelligence purposes and to correctional institutions regarding certain disclosures on inmates.

Some disclosures are permitted by the Privacy Rule, yet must be included in an accounting. Examples of these are disclosures by law, where a patient's permission is not required. Another example is a disclosure of identifiable information for research, for which an Institutional Review Board (IRB) or Privacy Board has waived the patient's authorization.

The first consideration on who should account for a misuse of records is if it is a business associate of the covered entity misusing the records. In that case, either the covered entity or the business associate is required to provide the accounting of what information they inappropriately disclose.

If the covered entity made a disclosure permitted by the Privacy Rule, and the person who received the information redisclosed the information, the covered entity does not have to account for the redisclosure. The person who received the information is then responsible for how the information is used or misused. If the person who receives the protected health information is also part of a covered entity, the requirement falls to the covered entity who makes the inappropriate disclosure to account for a disclosure not permitted by the Privacy Rule.

Finally, although an incidental disclosure does not have to be included in an accounting, an accidental disclosure by the covered entity should be. An accidental disclosure is a disclosure not permitted by the HIPAA Privacy Rule but made because of an error or through neglect.

References

Department of Health and Human Services. 45 CFR § 164.528(g).

Scenario 62

Do patients have to sign an authorization to obtain their own records?

 State and federal laws

KEY WORDS TO SEARCH: consent, authorization

If state law requires a written consent or authorization from the patient before providing the records, then an authorization should be obtained. A covered entity is also permitted by the HIPAA Privacy Rule to establish its own policies in this regard.

Absent state laws to the contrary, the HIPAA Privacy Rule has no requirement that patients sign an authorization to obtain their own records.

There may be practical or procedural reasons, however, to request that an individual provide a written request. A request in writing may be the only way to verify the identity of the requestor when the individual is not making the request in person. A written request is one method for the requestor to provide additional information or a signature to compare to information on file. Also, there may be a need to document the authority of a personal representative who is requesting the records of someone else. Such a request, however, does not have to meet the requirements of a HIPAA-compliant authorization; therefore, a handwritten request from a patient with sufficient information to identify what they are requesting and who they are should be sufficient for the covered entity to release the records.

References

Department of Health and Human Services. 45 CFR §§164.502(a), 164.514(h).

Scenario 63

What records, besides medical records, must we provide for individuals upon their request?

The HIPAA Privacy Rule normally gives individuals access to certain types of the covered entity's records, but not all. These records are called designated record sets in the Privacy Rule. To be considered a designated record set, the record set must meet three criteria:

- The record set must identify the individual.
- The record set must be maintained by the covered entity.
- The covered entity must use or have used the records to make decisions about the individual.

Usually, these records relate directly to the type of services the covered entity provides; for example, in the case of a healthcare provider, medical and billing records are the usual type of record. A health plan, on the other hand, has enrollment, payment, claims adjunction, and case management records. However, these are not the only record sets that may meet the three stated criteria; therefore, it is important that a covered entity review all identifiable record sets to see whether they need to be considered designated record sets. Fortunately, if information is duplicated in systems, such as a source laboratory system that interfaces to a clinical health record, the most complete record can be selected.

A large and complex covered entity often has multiple designated record sets. The Privacy Rule has a requirement that the covered entity maintain a list of designated record sets and a list of contact persons, or departments, who can provide access to them.

This list of designated record sets is rarely a static list, because new electronic systems may replace paper, or a new electronic system may replace a legacy system. As long as the information is maintained by the covered entity, the individual may request it. Therefore, it is important to also keep information about legacy systems or archived paper records during the time these records are retained.

References

Department of Health and Human Services. 45 CFR §§164.501, 164.524.

Scenario 64

Do we have to provide a copy of the Notice of Privacy Practices to patients every time we provide care for them?

A patient has a right to a Notice of Privacy Practices as defined in the HIPAA Privacy Rule. The notice has to be available, upon request, at the site of service for all direct healthcare providers.

A healthcare provider has to provide the notice no later than the date of the first service delivery, including a service delivered electronically, or as soon as possible in an emergency treatment situation. The notice must be posted in an area where individuals who seek services can read it. If the provider has a Web site, the notice content needs to be posted there as well. The notice can even be provided via email.

After that first provision of service, there is no requirement to provide a notice every time a patient receives services. Even when the notice is revised, the Privacy Rule only requires that the updated notice be posted and available to individuals at the physical delivery site of the healthcare provider.

Of course, the hardest part for the healthcare provider may be to know if the patient is receiving services the first time on this visit, or if it is a subsequent service and the notice has already been provided. If there is an electronic way to track the provision of the first notice and the acknowledgment from the patient that they were offered the notice, there is no need to provide a copy of the notice every time a service is provided.

References

Department of Health and Human Services. 45 CFR § 164.520.

Scenario 65

Do we have to provide the patient access to records from other providers if we include them in our medical record?

 State and federal laws

KEY WORDS TO SEARCH: medical records

The HIPAA Privacy Rule defines protected health information as any individually identifiable information which is created *or received by* a covered entity and related to the past, present, or future physical or mental health or condition of an individual or the provision of healthcare to the individual, or the payment for that care.

The Privacy Rule also defines a designated record set as a group of records that is *maintained by* or *for* a covered entity that includes protected health information and is *used in any way by the covered entity to make decisions about the individual.*

When other healthcare providers provide records, it is done to ensure the continuity of care for the individual. These copies often contain critical information about the prior care of the patient, and they are reviewed by the treating physician in order to make decisions about the current care of the patient.

Many covered entities either include the whole file or copies as part of the covered entity's record, with the assumption that the treating physician has used some or all of the records to decide how to treat the patient. Or, the treating physician is asked to review the copies and keep that which is pertinent to the current care of the patient, and these copies are included with an existing record.

Any copies that are included with the records of the individual are, therefore, considered part of the individual's designated record set. They were received by the covered entity, they are maintained by the covered entity, and they are used by the covered entity to make decisions about the individual.

Note that the term *designated record set* is applied to records to which the Privacy Rule establishes that a patient has certain rights, including rights of access and rights to request amendment. Besides medical records, it includes many types of records the covered entity may maintain and is not synonymous with "the legal medical record."

References

Department of Health and Human Services. 45 CFR §§160.103, 164.501.

Scenario 66

How soon do we have to provide patients copies of their own records? How soon do we have to provide records to other requestors?

 State and federal laws

KEY WORDS TO SEARCH: time to produce records, production of records

The HIPAA Privacy Rule establishes a timeframe for the production of records to individuals or their personal representatives.

The Privacy Rule does not establish timeframes for the production of records for treatment, payment, healthcare operations, or in response to an authorization from the patient to disclose information to another party. These timeframes may be established in state law, or there may be other reasons the records have to be provided by a certain timeframe. For example, record copies to be produced in response to a civil subpoena usually have to be provided in a designated time period. Some payor requests must be provided in the stated timeframe, or payment will be denied for the care.

Unless a state or federal law or regulation shortens the timeframe to provide copies or access at an individual's request, the covered entity has 30 days to provide copies or access to the individual or to his or her personal representative. When there is an issue, such as the record is not complete or cannot be found, the covered entity can obtain one 30-day extension if they inform the individual in writing for the reasons for the delay and when they expect to provide the records.

A covered entity may take an additional 30 days if the records are maintained off site.

References

Department of Health and Human Services. 45 CFR §164.524.

Scenario 67

Can we give patients copies of their records on a CD rather than on paper?

The patient can be provided a copy of his or her records, as long as he or she requests a CD and agrees to have the copies of his or her records provided on a CD or other electronic media instead of on paper. The HIPAA Privacy Rule states that the covered entity must provide individuals with their information in the form that is requested by the individuals, if it is readily producible in the requested format. The covered entity can certainly decide, along with the individual, the easiest and least expensive way to provide the copies they request.

However, if the individual informs the covered entity that he or she cannot read the records on a CD, the records must be provided on paper.

References

Department of Health and Human Services. 45 CFR §164.524(c)(2).

Scenario 68

When should we honor restriction requests?

 State or federal laws

KEY WORDS TO SEARCH: limitations of access

The HIPAA Privacy Rule allows individuals the right to request a restriction or limitation on how much of their record is used or disclosed for treatment, payment, or healthcare operations. They can also request that certain individuals be prevented from accessing their records. Finally, they can request that discussions about their care not be held with family members or friends.

The difficulty most covered entities have in granting these restriction requests is that the granting of a restriction becomes legally binding on the covered entity. In a large, complex healthcare environment, it is difficult to interrupt the flow of information for treatment, payment, or healthcare operations, because this flow is well established in procedures and systems. Providers may have different ways of dealing with family members, and, although the providers should ask patients if they want family members involved, in some cases, the provider does not have access to the patient and is making a judgment call on what information to disclose. The provider may, by accident, communicate information that violates the patient's request for a restriction. Also, in electronic record systems, it is sometimes impossible to restrict the access of a single individual to a single record.

There is an additional complication when patients make restriction requests of front line employees or providers because either these employees or providers do not understand the legal ramifications of the agreement to the covered entity, or they fail to understand the broader impact of their promise. The covered entity needs to educate all front line staff and providers in the appropriate process to follow when a restriction request is made. This process usually involves the patient submitting the request, in writing, to the privacy office or other designated department. There needs to be a defined process in which an individual or group reviews the request and in turn, agrees or does not agree with the restriction and responds to the patient with the decision.

Common practice by covered entities is not to agree to the restriction because of the legal implications to the covered entity should the restriction be violated. Instead, if there are valid reasons why the patient requests the restriction, covered entities implement steps in an attempt to restrict the information as best as their systems and processes allow. The covered entity responds to the patient by describing the measures it has taken but does not guarantee that the information is protected against incidental or accidental disclosure.

A few restriction requests are agreed to by a covered entity because the circumstances allow the restriction to be easily granted, such as a request that a record that is kept only on paper be maintained in a locked file, is self pay, and is single encounter. The other reason a request may be agreed to may be when there is a danger to the patient, in which case extraordinary measures, such as a permanent alias or creation of an entirely paper record instead of an electronic record, may be justified.

References

Department of Health and Human Services. 45 CFR §§ 164.510(b), 164.522(a).

Scenario 69

Do electronic disclosures mandated by state law have to be included in the accounting of disclosures?

 State and federal laws

KEY WORDS TO SEARCH: reportable disclosures to individuals, required or permitted reporting to state agencies, and public health reporting

The HIPAA Privacy Rule establishes that an individual can request that the covered entity give an accounting of all disclosures made concerning the individual's protected health information. Included in the accounting of disclosures are disclosures by law, for which the individual does not authorize the disclosure.

There are some who interpret disclosures to state-mandated data collection efforts to be disclosures for healthcare operations, both because it is a requirement for the covered entity to maintain its licensure and because the information is summarized and provided to the covered entity to make business decisions. When this is the case, there should be a memorandum of understanding or a business associate agreement with the state agency involved in order to cover the disclosure, because the agency is then functioning as a business associate. These types of disclosures do not need to be in an accounting, because they are for healthcare operations.

However, if there is no healthcare operations purpose for the disclosure, it is often a disclosure required by law. If public health law mandates the disclosure, the covered entity should determine if a limited data set might be used to meet the requirements of the law. In that case, the covered entity should obtain a data use agreement or equivalent with the state agency. Disclosures of limited data sets do not have to be included in an accounting of disclosures.

If the information is an identifiable data set, information about the disclosure by law must be included in an accounting of disclosures provided to the individual upon request. For repetitive disclosures to the same entity for the same reason, the covered entity is permitted to include the name of the entity who received the information, what information was disclosed, and the frequency of the disclosure, or the interval of time it is disclosed, such as, quarterly, or the number of disclosures made during the requested accounting period. The date of the last disclosure should be given to the individual.

References

Department of Health and Human Services. 45 CFR §§ 164.506, 164.512, 164.518, 164.528(g).

Scenario 70

Do Drug and Alcohol Regulations still apply to treatment programs, or only HIPAA?

 Alcohol and substance abuse laws

KEY WORDS TO SEARCH: covered program

The federal government finalized regulations in 1987, in response to statutes that guarantee strict confidentiality protections to individuals receiving drug abuse or alcohol abuse treatment. These regulations apply to "Programs," which are defined as individuals or entities, other than a general medical care facility, who "hold themselves out" as providing alcohol or drug abuse diagnosis, treatment or referral for treatment, or medical staffs in general medical care facilities that have this as their role and are identified as such. The other criteria to meet the definition of a "Program" is that the individual or entity must receive federal funding. After passage of the Drug Addiction Act in 2000, the definition of "Program" was interpreted to extend to individual physicians who obtain a special DEA waiver to use buprenorphine medications in their private practice to treat opioid addiction. Examples of programs provided in the regulation include: treatment or rehabilitation programs, methadone clinics, employee assistance programs (EAP), programs within general hospitals or schools, and private practitioners.

The HIPAA Privacy Rule, on the other hand, has different and broader criteria that define which individuals or entities are considered "covered entities." In general, the Privacy Rule applies to healthcare providers, health plans, healthcare clearinghouses, and Medicare Part D pharmacy plans. These entities must also be using the HIPAA-covered transactions to engage in billing or related functions.

In order to determine which regulations apply, the individual or entity must determine if they fit in one classification only, or both.

HIPAA does not replace other laws regarding the privacy of health records or the access to his or her health records by an individual, except in certain situations. When both the Drug and Alcohol Regulations and the Privacy Rules cover a program, the program must meet both regulations. In general, the Drug and Alcohol Regulations set a higher standard for patient privacy, and must be followed instead of the Privacy Rule. However, the main areas that the Privacy Rule will impose additional requirements are in the area of content of privacy notice, agreements with outside organizations, consent form revocation procedures, authorization content, research, and administrative requirements. Within the Department of Health and Human Services, the Substance Abuse and Mental Health Services Administration (SAMHSA) oversees the Drug and Alcohol Regulation implementation, while the Office for Civil Rights oversees the Privacy Rule implementation.

References

Department of Health and Human Services. 45 CFR § §160.103, 160.202, 42 CFR §§ 2.11, 2.12(b), (e);The Drug Addiction Treatment Act of 2000 (DATA 2000), Title XXXV, Section 3502 of the Children's Health Act of 2000; The Confidentiality Of Alcohol and Drug Abuse Patient Records Regulation and the HIPAA Privacy Rule: Implications For Alcohol and Substance Abuse Programs. Available online from http://www.hipaa.samhsa.gov/Part2ComparisonClearedTOC.htm

Scenario 71

Do we have to provide copies of employee access logs to a patient?

 State and federal laws

KEY WORDS TO SEARCH: identity theft, breach reporting

Access logs, also known as audit trails, are chronological records of system and user activities in electronic records. Access logs, depending on how they are constructed, may cover creating or deleting, access to, or editing of electronic records and are internal monitoring tools for the covered entity.

The HIPAA Privacy Rule establishes that an individual be able to request an accounting of all disclosures made of the individual's protected health information by the covered entity. There are some exceptions: treatment, payment, and healthcare operations do not have to be included in an accounting of disclosures.

Access logs generally cover the routine activities of treatment, payment, and healthcare operations. They are often voluminous and cryptic. If an employee uses his or her access rights to make disclosures not permitted by the Privacy Rule, such an inappropriate use or disclosure may be discovered by a review of an access log by the covered entity. Such an inappropriate disclosure by the employee should be documented as part of an accounting of disclosures if the individual requests an accounting. However, an accounting of disclosures is required to have certain contents, specifically, records of certain "disclosures"—not "uses"—therefore, it does not require evidence of appropriate or inappropriate access to the individual's records.

There is no requirement in the Privacy Rule that gives individuals a right to a copy of access logs relating to the activity of their records. If a covered entity provides copies of or access to these logs, it should be based on policy, not as a requirement by law.

References

Department of Health and Human Services. 45 CFR § 164.528(g).

Scenario 72

Are we required by HIPAA to notify patients of accidental disclosures?

 State and federal laws

KEY WORDS TO SEARCH: privacy breach notification requirements, identity theft

An accidental disclosure is a disclosure made because of error or neglect and is not permitted by the HIPAA Privacy Rule. As such, it may need to be part of an accounting of disclosures, as it is not a permitted disclosure for treatment, payment, healthcare operations, by authorization, or otherwise exempt from the accounting of disclosures.

Therefore, when a patient requests an accounting of disclosures, the information would be available to the individual.

There is no specific requirement in the Privacy Rule that demands that the covered entity notify the individual of disclosures of personal health information in violation of the Privacy Rule. However, the covered entity does have a responsibility to mitigate any harmful effect the covered entity knows about that may have resulted from a violation of the Privacy Rule.

Each time an accidental disclosure occurs, the covered entity should review the risks to the patient. Much depends on the content of the disclosed materials and who received the information. If the patient is well known and the information contained in the accidental disclosure is sensitive information, it may be in the covered entity's best interest to inform the patient about what occurred. In addition, if the information included social security numbers, credit card numbers, or PINs, the patient may be at risk for identity theft.

Therefore, although it is not specifically required by the Privacy Rule, notification of the patient may be considered as part of the mitigation process or because other state or federal notification laws require the covered entity to do so.

References

Department of Health and Human Services. 45 CFR §§ 164.528, 164.530(f).

Scenario 73

What should we do when a laptop with protected health information is stolen or lost?

 State and federal laws

KEY WORDS TO SEARCH: privacy breach notification requirements, identity theft

If a laptop or storage media that contains protected heath information is lost or stolen, the covered entity must review the risks to individuals whose information was contained in the laptop.

The covered entity should have established an incident response team and/or process to call upon in this situation, as required in the HIPAA Security Rule. These teams often include individuals with expertise in information systems, risk management, law and regulations, public relations, and human resources. The covered entity must first attempt to determine the information that was contained on the laptop. Some of the content may be found by examining backups made by the laptop user to internal servers, reviewing system activity logs, stored queries, and use of e-mail by the user. The user of the laptop should be interviewed to determine if there was a password protecting the laptop, the circumstances of the theft, and what the person recalls as being stored on the laptop.

The assessment of risk to the individuals whose information is contained on the laptop depends on the degree and type of information that was stored on the laptop that is individually identifiable. If the information contains sensitive diagnosis information, or if the information includes social security numbers or credit card numbers or PINs, the risk to the individuals becomes significant if the person who stole the laptop decides to publish the information or use it for identity theft.

If the names of individuals whose information is contained in the stolen laptop can be identified by the covered entity, the theft of the laptop should be included in information provided for the accounting of disclosures. Therefore, if an individual requests an accounting of disclosures, the information would be available to the individual.

There is not a specific requirement in the HIPAA Privacy Rule that demands the covered entity to notify the individual of disclosures of personal health information in violation of the Privacy Rule. However, the covered entity does have a responsibility to mitigate any harmful effect the covered entity knows about that may have resulted from a violation of the Privacy Rule. It has become common practice to offer credit monitoring services to individuals when there has been a breach of information that could be used for identity theft.

Therefore, although the Privacy Rule does not specifically require it, notification of the patient may be considered part of the mitigation process, because other state or federal notification laws require the covered entity to do so, or because the covered entity decides that individuals may be at risk from the theft or loss of their information.

References

Department of Health and Human Services. 45 CFR §§ 164.308(a)(6)(i), 164.528, 164.530(f).

Scenario 74

What would be considered a compound authorization and, therefore, invalid?

 State and federal laws

KEY WORDS TO SEARCH: consent, authorization

The HIPAA Privacy Rule defines the contents of authorizations which are valid under the Privacy Rule and which a covered entity may use as permission to disclose protected health information. The writers of the Privacy Rule intended that individuals not be coerced into disclosing their protected health information, and so an authorization generally is a separate document that only addresses the use or disclosure of the individual's protected health information. These authorizations can be compound documents, according to the Privacy Rule, only in the following situations:

♦ An authorization to disclose protected health information for research may be combined with consent for research. However, if the individual must sign the authorization to be included in a clinical trial, for example, and the researcher also requests the ability to use treatment information created prior to the clinical trial, a compound consent and authorization may be used to grant permission for the clinical trial's use of the information, but a second and separate authorization with no conditions is required for the researcher to access the prior treatment records of the individual.

♦ An authorization to disclose protected health information included in psychotherapy notes may be combined to disclose the information for multiple purposes, but cannot include other types of records.

♦ An authorization to disclose protected health information, excluding psychotherapy notes about an individual from one set of records, may be combined with an authorization to disclose information about the individual from another set of records, or from a single set of records for multiple purposes, as long as there are no conditions included in the authorization wording.

An authorization may not be combined with consent for treatment or assignment of benefits. The covered entity is permitted to obtain a separate authorization with conditions for treatment, payment, or eligibility for benefits, as long as the conditions are clearly defined for the individual.

An authorization may not be part of a Notice of Privacy Practices.

An authorization may not be part of or include wording regarding any other legal written permission to use or disclose protected health information. Under that definition, an authorization that includes revocation wording, such as "I hereby revoke all prior written authorizations . . ." or restrictions "I prohibit the facility from using any employed copy service to process this request . . ." would be a compound authorization and, therefore, invalid under the Privacy Rule.

References

Department of Health and Human Services. 45 CFR § 164.508(b); Department of Health and Human Services. 2000. Final Rule: Standards for the Privacy of Individually Identifiable Health Information. *Federal Register* 65(250): 82517, 82621, 82658.

Scenario 75

How do healthcare providers know when it is okay to talk to family members about a patient?

The HIPAA Privacy Rule is very specific about the situations in which a patient has the right to verbally approve disclosures. If a patient is able to express a preference regarding a disclosure to family or friends, the patient needs to be given the opportunity to agree or object. When a patient does not speak up, his or her agreement can be assumed. An element of professional judgment can be used in these circumstances as well; if a spouse is present with the patient, and the patient has never expressed a concern about the spouse being present, the provider can assume it is okay to speak about the patient. If the patient is not able to express a preference, it is up to professional judgment to determine whether the disclosure is in the best interest of the individual and the information to be shared is something the other person needs to know in the circumstance.

As a practical suggestion, a healthcare provider who does not know who visitors are should ask them to leave the patient's room before talking with a patient who is able to respond. The patient can then be asked whether he or she wishes any of the visitors to be invited back in for the discussion. This procedure will cause the patient less pressure to make a decision in front of a group.

If the patient is unable to consent, the healthcare provider should still ask all of the visitors to step out, then ask if one of them is the patient's personal representative or whether any of them will be directly involved in the patient's care. The healthcare provider may ask questions about the visitors' relationships or what services they provide for the patient in order to determine the amount of information the family or friends may need.

References

Department of Health and Human Services. 45 CFR §164.510(b).

Scenario 76

How can family passwords or codes be implemented to verify identity?

 State and federal laws

KEY WORDS TO SEARCH: mental health therapy, behavioral health treatment

 Alcohol and substance abuse laws

Federal Drug and Alcohol Treatment Program Record Regulations require any patient receiving Program services to sign a consent or authorization prior to disclosure of information identifying the patient as receiving these treatment services. This applies even to family members involved in the patient's care.

The HIPAA Privacy Rule allows a covered entity to disclose information to family or friends if the patient agrees. Technically, the covered entity does not have to verify the identity of a family member or friend that the patient has designated as being involved in his or her care. However, when a family member or friend is calling in on the phone to obtain information about the patient, it is very difficult determine if this is the family member the patient designated to receive the protected health information. Patients are not always able to be consulted when the family member calls.

Some covered entities have been successful in using passwords in this situation. A patient is offered the opportunity to choose a password, which is available in the patient's record. Staff members are trained to verify the password before disclosing more than the general status of the patient. Or, the account number is used as the password for family and friends, as it changes for every admission. Patients are responsible for sharing the password with the family or friends they wish to have access to further information about their condition. Patients should be encouraged to assign new passwords for each admission, especially if the patient chooses different members of the family to be involved in subsequent admissions, or in case family members shared the earlier password with others.

This is a good solution for facilities that are located in retirement areas where the patient's children may be geographically distant. However, unless required by state or other federal laws, the facility should be cautious in writing its policy regarding use of these passwords, in that the policy should be written to allow provider judgment in addition to what is stated in these documents.

References

Department of Health and Human Services. 45 CFR §§164.510(b), 164.514(h)(1).

Scenario 77

Can parents of adults set up appointments?

The HIPAA Privacy Rule allows a covered entity to disclose information to family or friends, or even other persons who may not be friends but are assisting the individual, if the individual agrees to the disclosure. The information disclosed by the covered entity has to be relevant and limited to the reason the person is involved.

The covered entity needs a reasonable assurance of the preference of the individual, such as a letter or other signed document. Or, the healthcare provider can assume the individual's permission based on the circumstances of the request.

In the case of a parent calling in to obtain an appointment for an adult child, or a wife calling a health plan to discuss the details of her husband's bill, the covered entity can share relevant protected health information. The parent should provide sufficient details about the adult child to satisfy the covered entity that the parent is involved in the adult child's care. It is also reasonable to expect the wife to provide the husband's health plan number and birth date, or other identifier, before disclosing the information.

References

Department of Health and Human Services. 45 CFR §164.510(b). Department of Health and Human Services, Office for Civil Rights. Your Frequently Asked Questions On Privacy. 1067. Available online from http://www.dhhs.gov/ocr/hipaa/.

Scenario 78

Does communication with family members require authorization from the patient?

 State and federal laws

KEY WORDS TO SEARCH: mental health therapy, behavioral health treatment

 Alcohol and substance abuse laws

Federal Drug and Alcohol Treatment Program Record Regulations require any patient receiving Program services to sign a consent or authorization prior to disclosure of information identifying the patient as receiving these treatment services. This applies even to family members involved in the patient's care.

The HIPAA Privacy Rule allows the covered entity to communicate with families as long as certain conditions are met. The covered entity must have verbal or implied confirmation from the patient. The covered entity must also be able to determine in the situation how much the family member is involved in the care of the patient. The extent of his or her involvement in the care determines how much information the family member can be given about the patient; in other words, the information shared must be relevant to the role he or she is playing in the patient's care. Therefore, when these conditions are met, there is not a requirement for an authorization.

This is the easiest situation in which to determine patient preference, but what about when patients are not able express their wishes?

The Privacy Rule invokes professional judgment in that case, with the continuing condition that the covered entity provides only information relevant to the family's involvement in the care of the patient. In order to assist in this decision, some covered entities allow the patient to give a password to the family, who must then know the password to receive information. Others have created "Patient/Family Contacts" documents in which patients may include names of family members they wish to have further information. These documents do not necessarily meet the requirements of the HIPAA compliant authorization, unless the patient is intending to disclose copies of records to these family members. Unless required by state or other federal laws, the facility should be cautious in writing its policy regarding use of these documents or codes; however, the policy should be written to allow provider judgment in addition to what is stated on these documents.

References

Department of Health and Human Services. 45 CFR §164.510(b).

Scenario 79

May another person pick up copies of records on an adult patient without an authorization?

 State and federal laws

KEY WORDS TO SEARCH: mental health therapy, behavioral health treatment

 Alcohol and substance abuse laws

Federal Drug and Alcohol Treatment Program Record Regulations require any patient receiving Program services to sign a consent or authorization prior to disclosure of information identifying the patient as receiving these treatment services. This applies even to family members involved in the patient's care.

The HIPAA Privacy Rule allows the disclosure of some forms of protected health information to other persons when the individual is not present. In those cases, the Privacy Rule allows the covered entity to use professional judgment and infer it is in the individual's best interest to have another person pick up prescriptions, radiology films, or other medical supplies.

However, there are two other criteria that must be met in this situation. The information must be relevant to the involvement of this other person in the care or payment of the care of the patient. Second, disclosing these records must be a common healthcare industry practice.

To provide copies of medical records to someone else does not generally meet these two criteria. The extent of the information included in a medical record copy usually exceeds what this person needs to know. In addition, picking up another person's medical records without an authorization is not a common practice.

Why would a provider consider allowing another person to obtain even limited copies of the protected health information of an individual? The Privacy Rule permits another person to pick up radiology images with the idea that it is a service to an ill, infirm, or unavailable patient, but the patient needs these for follow-up care with another physician. However, radiology images are rarely without other accompanying information; film folders contain transcribed interpretations, and even digital images burned to a disk have the interpretations included as well. If the provider requires authorization before disclosing the interpretations that are included with the radiology images, often it becomes a barrier to patient care and a major dissatisfier to the individual.

In this situation, the healthcare provider needs to decide whether the risks to patient privacy outweigh the barriers to patient care imposed by following the letter of the Privacy Rule. The healthcare provider should carefully document the risks and benefits before deciding to implement a decision that may be in conflict with the Privacy Rule. Also, the provider should implement any steps that will reduce the risks of inappropriate disclosure. For example, the provider may ask the person picking up the images to show proof of identity and to sign an affidavit stating that he or she is picking the information up on behalf of the patient for the purpose of a follow-up appointment. The provider may also want to verbally confirm the appointment with another provider. The clerks should be instructed that if the purpose is not continuing care, or if there is doubt in a particular situation, an authorization should be required prior to allowing the person possession of the films and reports.

There are other situations that are similar. For example, a person with family insurance coverage may need to pick up a summary of the family's prescriptions from a pharmacy to submit to a health plan for reimbursement. In this situation, the information is limited, as is often common practice in healthcare settings; therefore, the requirements of the Privacy Rule are met.

References

Department of Health and Human Services. 45 CFR §164.510(b).

Scenario 80

Can messages be left with family or on answering machines to remind patients of appointments?

Alcohol and substance abuse laws

Federal Drug and Alcohol Treatment Program Record Regulations allow the Program to communicate with a patient receiving services. No message left for a patient, however, should ever identify the Program as a source. If patients wish to have their family or friends know about their treatment, they must sign a consent or authorization that allows the disclosure to those specific individuals.

The HIPAA Privacy Rule allows a covered entity to communicate with individuals about the individual's own healthcare or payment of that care. This includes leaving messages with family or on answering machines. The constraints the Privacy Rule imposes about leaving messages are that they are limited to the minimum necessary information for the purpose, and, when the individual expresses a preference for the method of communication, the covered entity should accommodate the request if it is reasonable. When messages are left with family, they should be limited to the information relevant to their involvement with that care. Finally, if a covered entity intends to contact individuals for this purpose, they need to include a statement about this activity in their Notice of Privacy Practices.

To ensure that the information left on answering machines or with family members is appropriate, it is best to develop a script in advance to keep the content of the message consistent. Messages should be as limited as possible but still meet the purpose of the communication: "This is Jan at phone number . . . . This is to confirm our appointment this week at . . ." or "Please have . . . call me; he asked me to contact him."

Personal mobile phones provide more opportunities to talk directly with the individual, and messages left in a mailbox provided as part of the mobile phone service are generally more secure, as most individuals do not typically share mobile phones.

Some covered entities collect the individual's mobile phone number or ask the individual to designate how the covered entity may communicate private messages to him or her. Or, the individual can designate whether he or she wishes to have messages left. If the individual designates these preferences, a covered entity must make reasonable attempts to accommodate the request.

References

Department of Health and Human Services. 45 CFR§§164.510(b)(3), 164.522(b), 164.520(b)(iii)(A); Department of Health and Human Services, Office for Civil Rights. Your Frequently Asked Questions On Privacy. 198. Available online from http://www. dhhs.gov/ocr/hipaa/.

Scenario 81

Can pre-procedure instructions for a patient be left with family when the patient cannot be reached?

The HIPAA Privacy Rule allows a healthcare provider to communicate with individuals about their own healthcare. An important part of that communication may include instructions the patient must follow prior to an outpatient procedure. Examples of these instructions are to refrain from eating or drinking a particular number of hours before the procedure, to arrange to have someone accompany him or her and drive the patient home after the procedure, or to avoid taking certain medications prior to the procedure. These are critical communications for the treatment and safety of the patient, and, as such, the risk to the patient's privacy in making the communication should not be the healthcare provider's main concern.

The ideal, of course, is for this information to be provided to the patient directly, but this is not always possible. Another option is to obtain information from patients at the time of setting the appointment as to the best way to contact them to give them the instructions. If time allows, the instructions can be mailed.

Otherwise, the healthcare provider may leave a message for the patient to call the provider back, indicating the urgency of the return call. However, this does not always work, either, because the patient may not retrieve the message, or the provider who can provide the instructions may not be available when the patient calls back.

If other communication options are not workable, and the patient cannot be reached, the only other option available may be to leave the instructions on a message machine or communicate the instructions to a family member who agrees to pass them on to the patient. The healthcare provider can assume from this situation that the family member is sufficiently involved in the care of the patient to receive this information, and that the disclosure is in the best interest of the patient.

References

Department of Health and Human Services. 45 CFR §164.510(b)(3); Department of Health and Human Services, Office for Civil Rights. Your Frequently Asked Questions On Privacy. 198, 488. Available online from http://www.dhhs.gov/ocr/hipaa/.

Scenario 82

When can a physician give patients' names and contact information to a researcher?

State and federal laws

KEY WORDS TO SEARCH: research, research subject recruitment

Alcohol and substance abuse laws

Federal Drug and Alcohol Treatment Program Regulations permit the disclosure of information for research with consent by the individual. They also permit the disclosure of patient identifying information to researchers, as long as the researchers agree to de-identify the information before disclosing it to anyone else, or to only disclose identifiable results back to the Program. Finally, a researcher may contact individuals who have been treated in a Program as part of a research project only if the contact does not indicate the individuals have received treatment in a Program.

Covered healthcare providers can discuss research projects with their patients under the HIPAA Privacy Rule. This is considered a treatment-related communication. The healthcare provider can give the patient information concerning how to contact the researcher, and the patient then may make the contact.

One of the following must be done in order for the healthcare provider to directly disclose the identity and contact information of a patient to a researcher:

First, the provider can obtain an authorization to disclose the contact information of patients to the researcher when patients decide they wish to participate in the research.

Second, when the healthcare provider and the researcher are part of the same covered entity, the healthcare provider may give the contact information to the researcher. The researcher is permitted to contact the patient on behalf of the covered entity for the healthcare operations' purpose of providing information about treatment alternatives. Or, if the covered entity, to which both the healthcare provider and the researcher belong, has engaged a business associate to recruit subjects, the healthcare provider may give the contact information to the business associate.

Finally, when the researcher is not part of the same covered entity, the healthcare provider must obtain documentation from the researcher that he or she has obtained a partial waiver of authorization from an Institutional Review Board for the purpose of subject recruitment. This waiver should describe the information the healthcare provider is allowed to disclose to the researcher. Disclosures made based on a waiver need to be included in an accounting of disclosures, should the patient request one.

References

Department of Health and Human Services. 45 CFR §§ 164.501, 164.506, 164.512(i), 164.528; 42 CFR § 2.52; DHHS National Institutes of Health. Clinical Research and the HIPAA Privacy Rule. Available online from http://privacyruleandresearch.nih.gov/clin_research.asp

Scenario 83

Do inmates have privacy rights under HIPAA?

State and federal laws

KEY WORDS TO SEARCH: inmate, in custody, in prison, DNA testing, HIV testing

Alcohol and substance abuse laws
Drug and Alcohol Treatment Programs have special rules about irrevocable consents when a patient's participation in the treatment program is mandatory and is a condition of a sentence or imprisonment. This means that an inmate may have no right to revoke an authorization in these circumstances.

Individually identifiable information about inmates is included in the protections of the HIPAA Privacy Rule. However, an inmate has fewer rights under the Privacy Rule than an individual who is not an inmate. An inmate is a person who is incarcerated in, or is otherwise confined to a correctional institution. A correctional institution is a prison, jail, reformatory, work farm, detention center, or halfway house, or any other similar institution designed for the confinement or rehabilitation of criminal offenders. It also includes transitional homes, and other facilities in which inmates are required by law to remain for correctional reasons and from which inmates are not allowed to leave. This also covers individuals who are confined to psychiatric institutions for correctional reasons and who are not allowed to leave; however, it does not apply to disclosure of information about individuals in psychiatric institutions for treatment purposes only, who are not there due to a crime or under a mandate from the criminal justice system. A person is no longer considered an inmate when released on probation, parole, supervised release, or is otherwise not in legal custody. After an inmate is released, he or she assumes the same rights as any other individual. An inmate's rights are restricted in the following areas:

♦ Inmates do not have a right to a Notice of Privacy Practices.

♦ Inmates can request access to their protected health information, but the correctional institution may deny that request if granting it would jeopardize the health, safety, security, custody, or rehabilitation of the individuals or other inmates, or the safety of correctional employees.

♦ A correctional institution may be provided protected health information about an inmate if it is necessary for the treatment of the inmate, the safety of employees or other inmates, or the maintenance of good order in the correctional institution. Disclosures for these purposes do not have to be included in an accounting of disclosures.

♦ Finally, state or federal laws may mandate medical testing on an inmate, such as HIV or DNA testing, or treatment for substance abuse. The inmate does not have the right to control the disclosure of these types of testing or treatment information.

References

Department of Health and Human Services. 45 CFR §§164.501, 164.512(k) 5, 164.520(a)(3); Department of Health and Human Services. 2000. Final Rule: Standards for the Privacy of Individually Identifiable Health Information. *Federal Register* 65(250): 82541; Department of Health and Human Services. 42 CFR § 2.35.

Scenario 84

If an individual has a power of attorney, is he or she a personal representative under HIPAA?

 State and federal laws

KEY WORDS TO SEARCH: personal representative, power of attorney, healthcare power of attorney, next of kin, and guardianship

In order to be considered a personal representative in the HIPAA Privacy Rule, a person must have authority to act on behalf of an individual under applicable law. The person can have a power of attorney and be considered a personal representative if two conditions are met. The power of attorney must give the person the right to make healthcare decisions about an individual, and the conditions to invoke the power of attorney must have been met.

For example, when an individual agrees that another person has power of attorney to make treatment decisions about him or her if they are comatose, then the person may exercise the rights of a personal representative. However, the rights to the protected health information of the individual by a personal representative are limited to only that information relevant to the healthcare decisions for the individual's treatment while in a coma. It would not permit the personal representative to access any and all records of the individual.

There are many types of powers of attorney. Some are limited to making financial decisions. If the power of attorney only grants rights over financial matters and not rights to make healthcare decisions about the individual, then the individual cannot be provided copies of the individual's medical records. However, if the person has financial power of attorney over the individual's assets and power to pay the individual's bills, and the conditions invoking the power of attorney are met, a health plan or a healthcare provider may disclose relevant payment and billing information to the person in order to get the individual's bills paid.

References

Department of Health and Human Services. 45 CFR §164.502(g); Department of Health and Human Services. 2000. Final Rule: Standards for the Privacy of Individually Identifiable Health Information. *Federal Register* 65(250): 82501

Scenario 85

Are the records of a deceased person protected under HIPAA?

Many times under state law, a deceased individual's records are no longer subject to physician-patient privilege. Also, research-related regulations do not protect a deceased individual's records, because these regulations apply to the protection of human subjects.

However, the HIPAA Privacy Rule extends the same protections to a deceased individual's records as to living individual's records, with some limited exceptions. The Privacy Rule as proposed originally stated that protections on deceased individual's protected health information would only extend for two years after death. However, the final Privacy Rule extends the protections to as long as the covered entity retains the records.

Research provisions in the Privacy Rule differ somewhat in dealing with decedent records. Research on decedent records is permitted if a researcher certifies that the records required are all on deceased patients. The researcher may be required to prove this by providing copies of death certificates.

Funeral directors may receive protected health information necessary to perform their duties for the deceased individual. The rights to access a deceased individual's records are transferred to the personal representative of the individual, usually the executor of the individual's estate.

References

Department of Health and Human Services. 45 CFR §§164.502(g), 164.512(i), 164.512(g); Department of Health and Human Services. 2000. Final Rule: Standards for the Privacy of Individually Identifiable Health Information. *Federal Register* 65(250): 82501

Scenario 86

What happens if patients request their records, but the records are lost?

 State and federal laws

KEY WORDS TO SEARCH: privacy breach notification requirements, identity theft, and retention of records

If an individual's records cannot be found, it is best to reconstruct the records as much as possible. Notify the risk management or the facility's malpractice insurance carrier of the loss, especially, when there is the possibility of litigation involving the individual.

In order to reconstruct the record, contact the unit or department where the individual received services, so that duplicated copies, if there are any, can be included in the record. Review itemized bills to determine the types of services rendered, to make sure that all departments who provided services for the patient have been contacted:

- ♦ Print out available reports if the reports are maintained electronically.

- ♦ Contact physicians or other providers to see if they have copies that cannot be produced from electronic storage.

- ♦ Obtain signatures on documents, unless electronic signatures are stored and can be reproduced.

- ♦ Ask a physician to re-dictate reports, as long as it is apparent from the dates on the document that this is a reconstruction or re-dictation.

It is recommended that documentation be added as part of the record as to: date of loss or discovery of loss; date of record reconstruction; documents duplicated from copies, documents reconstructed, or documents redictated.

Include a statement, such as: "This record is a replica of the original. The original has been reconstructed to the extent possible. For purposes of facility business, it is considered to be a complete record at this time. It will be replaced with the original upon recovery."

If individuals request copies of their own record, only copies of the replica can be provided. Provide a copy of the replica statement, as well. Technically, a covered entity is required by the HIPAA Privacy Rule to provide access to individuals to protected health information for as long as the information is retained by the covered entity, and if the record is lost, it cannot be provided, except as a replica. Therefore, the inability to provide the record is not a violation of the access rights included in the Privacy Rule. However, the covered entity may be guilty of not providing reasonable safeguards to protect the information. If there is a possibility that the record was stolen, mitigation for the individual may be in order. The covered entity may also be in violation of state or federal retention statutes.

References

Department of Health and Human Services. 45 CFR §§164.530, 164.524.

Scenario 87

Does a guarantor on a health insurance policy have a right to information on other dependents included on the policy?

 State and federal laws

KEY WORDS TO SEARCH: contracts, responsibility for payment

A guarantor, or a named insured, on a health insurance policy usually has some rights under state contract laws to be given proof that services were provided to dependents. Legally, the guarantor on an account may be responsible for payment of a bill.

To the extent that the named insured has dependents on the insurance policy, the named insured may be considered a personal representative for limited purposes, such as verifying the accuracy of payment or making decisions on disputed claims. A guarantor on an account may be provided limited information to prove that services were provided, such as an itemized statement. This individual would not be considered a personal representative in regards to other information, unless the person is a personal representative by law, such as a parent who has minor children.

In the case of domestic abuse or other threats to safety, a dependent on an insurance policy does have the right to request, and be granted, alternate methods of communication from a covered entity that may limit the information normally sent to the guarantor. Also, if a person is a threat to another individual, the covered entity may deny access to records because of the threat.

References

Department of Health and Human Services. 45 CFR §§164.502(g), 164.522(b). Department of Health and Human Services. 2000. Final Rule: Standards for the Privacy of Individually Identifiable Health Information. *Federal Register* 65(250): 82661.

SECTION VI

Treatment, Payment, and Healthcare Operations

This section deals with the myriad of activities that require an individual's information to be shared within and among covered entities.

Scenario 88

Are dates of admission protected health information?

State and federal laws

KEY WORDS TO SEARCH: consent, authorization

Alcohol and substance abuse laws

Federal Drug and Alcohol Treatment Program Regulations do not allow the Program to disclose that a patient has been treated in the Program, unless the patient has signed an authorization permitting the disclosure to be made.

The HIPAA Privacy Rule defines protected health information as individually identifiable health information. At first glance, dates of stay would not appear to be very identifiable; but HIPAA also defines dates related to the individual as one of the data elements that must be removed from a data set in order for it to be considered de-identified.

Prior to the implementation of the Privacy Rule, dates of admission were often disclosed to callers over the phone. Most of these callers were insurers, trying to verify the dates on a submitted claim. This disclosure to the patient's health insurer is still permitted under HIPAA, if the covered entity verifies the identity of the insurer. Disclosure of dates to other callers is permitted only when the disclosure falls within treatment, payment, healthcare operations, by authorization, or by law.

Just because a caller knows the patient's name when he or she calls, and the patient did not opt out of a facility directory, does not mean that dates of admission can be provided to the caller. The facility directory provisions in the Privacy Rule relate to visitors and callers being provided sufficient information to locate the patient while the patient is present in the facility and allow these persons to obtain general information about the patient's condition. Once a patient is discharged, the reason the limited directory information can be disclosed no longer exists.

By law, the patient is one of those who may receive the information. If the patient's identity can be confirmed in a phone call, it is permitted to disclose dates of admission to the patient.

References

Department of Health and Human Services. 45 CFR §§160.103, 164.510, 164.514, 164.502(a).

Scenario 89

Are authorizations required to disclose treatment information?

 State and federal laws

KEY WORDS TO SEARCH: consent, authorization

 Alcohol and substance abuse laws

Federal Drug and Alcohol Treatment Program Regulations require a signed authorization from a patient in order to disclose records to other treatment providers, except in emergency situations. Even in emergency situations, the information to be disclosed should be limited to the information necessary for the care.

An authorization may be required by a covered entity prior to disclosure of information for treatment in certain circumstances. Some state laws require a healthcare provider to obtain written consent or authorization from the patient before disclosing information for treatment purposes. Also, the HIPAA Privacy Rule permits the covered entity to require a written consent be signed before a treatment disclosure is made. Another treatment provider may have to meet the covered entity's policy for written consent in order to obtain the requested protected health information.

On the other hand, the HIPAA Privacy Rule has no requirement that a patient must sign an authorization to disclose information to another treatment provider who is caring for him or her.

Covered entities do have a requirement to establish the identity and the authority of the persons who are requesting protected health information, however. In the case of a treatment provider requesting records, this may be done by having the request for records on office letterhead with sufficient information to identify the patient (name, birth date) sent to the covered entity.

Further, minimum necessary requirements do not apply to treatment disclosures. The covered entity is free to disclose the information requested by the other healthcare provider. However, if it is unclear that the requestor of the information is a treatment provider, the covered entity should clarify the status of the requestor. Although there is not a requirement to obtain an authorization for treatment, it is not prohibited to ask for one when a covered entity is unsure of the identity of the requestor.

References

Department of Health and Human Services. 45 CFR §§164.502, 164.514(h); 42 CFR§§ 2.13, 2.31, 2.51.

Scenario 90

Are there ever external disclosures of personal health information (PHI) for healthcare operations?

 State and federal laws

KEY WORDS TO SEARCH: liability insurance, consent, and authorization

 Alcohol and substance abuse laws

Federal Drug and Alcohol Treatment Program Regulations permit the disclosure of information to an entity having direct administrative control over that program. However, redisclosure of identifiable patient information is generally not permitted unless the patient has signed a consent or authorization, or the external provider of services has entered into a qualified service organization agreement with the Program.

The HIPAA Privacy Rule allows a covered entity to use protected health information for a broad range of activities necessary for the covered entity to stay in business. These activities include quality improvement, credentialing, training, licensing, business planning, medical or legal services, resolution of internal grievances, as necessary for selling the business, and fundraising, just to name a few that are specifically listed in the Privacy Rule.

Many of these types of services are contracted out to other, noncovered entities. The writers of the Privacy Rule realized that covered entities would be extremely hampered if they could not use these types of businesses, as well as share the protected health information necessary for the service to be provided. However, the Secretary of Health and Human Services has no power to ensure that the protected health information shared with a business associate is protected by the Privacy Rule, in that the Secretary has no power to enforce the Privacy Rule over noncovered entities. However, the Secretary does have the power to require the covered entity to enter into agreements with noncovered entities, agreements that require the noncovered entity to provide the same protections to health information as apply to the covered entity. These are business associate agreements. The majority of the services provided by business associates are related to healthcare operations. A covered entity can, therefore, disclose protected health information to an external business associate for healthcare operations' purposes.

References

Department of Health and Human Services. 45 CFR §§ 164.501, 164.504; 42 CFR § 2.12(c)(4).

Scenario 91

May we give a copy of the complaint letter to the patient's health insurer who has been named as part of a complaint?

In deciding to share a copy of a complaint letter, several issues should be considered. First, is a complaint letter received by a covered entity protected health information? Such a letter would normally relate to the past or present provision of healthcare or the payment of the individual and, unless anonymous, would identify the individual. It also is received and maintained by the covered entity. Therefore, as long as the covered entity maintains a copy, it would be protected health information. It may also be considered part of a designated record set if used to make decisions about the care or payment for care of the individual.

Of course, if the entity who receives the complaint can contact the individual, the entity may ask the individual to send a copy of the complaint letter to the health insurer, or, alternatively, that the complainant sign an authorization for the letter to be disclosed to the health insurer. If the complainant cannot be reached for permission, there are still options to consider.

The receiving covered entity may de-identify the copy of the complaint, but this may limit the ability of the health insurer to investigate or respond. Alternatively, as the health insurer is a covered entity as well, there are circumstances in which it is permitted in the HIPAA Privacy Rule to share a patient's information for the healthcare operations of another covered entity. The first condition is that the patient needs to have received services from both entities.

The second condition that must be met is that the reason for the disclosure must fall within a subset of healthcare operations as defined in the Privacy Rule. The covered entity that has the letter must determine that the health insurer will use the information in the letter for quality improvement of the insurer's organization, or improvement of its performance as a health plan. A purpose that would not be appropriate would be to give the letter to the health insurer to help the insurer prepare for a legal case to be filed against the insurer.

Third, the information forwarded to the health insurer should be the minimum necessary for the purpose. Sending the entire letter may not be appropriate, but only the sections relevant to the complaint about the health insurer.

If the complaint is in regards to a breach of the Privacy Rule by the other covered entity, the individual should be encouraged to complain to the health insurer directly. The health insurer's Notice of Privacy Practices should contain information on how to contact the individual or office of the other covered entity to file a complaint.

References

Department of Health and Human Services. 45 CFR §§ 164.501, 164.506, 164.530, 164.520(c).

Scenario 92

Should a health insurer provide a copy of its entire eligibility file to a healthcare provider so insurance coverage can be verified when a patient comes for care?

State and federal laws

KEY WORDS TO SEARCH: liability insurance, consent, and authorization

Alcohol and substance abuse laws

Federal Drug and Alcohol Treatment Program Regulations require that a patient sign a consent or authorization before disclosures can be made for any payment purpose, including eligibility verification.

The HIPAA Privacy Rule permits healthcare providers and health plans to disclose protected health information for payment purposes. Determining the eligibility and coverage of the individual are considered payment activities.

However, the minimum necessary provisions apply to payment activities; a covered entity must try to limit the information necessary to accomplish the intended purpose of the disclosure.

A health insurer's eligibility file will include all of its members, not just the members who seek services with a single healthcare provider. Therefore, to disclose an entire eligibility file to a healthcare provider would exceed the minimum necessary standard, in that it would contain information on members prior to their seeking services with the healthcare provider.

A healthcare provider would be better off pursuing the use of a standard electronic transaction with the health plan that could verify eligibility and coverage of the individual by the health plan.

References

Department of Health and Human Services. 45 CFR §§ 164.501, 164.504, 45 CFR§ 162.1201, 42CFR § 2.12(c)(4).

Scenario 93

May we give copies of patients' records to a physician for his specialty certification?

Physicians who wish to obtain advanced certification are required to provide evidence of their experience and skills. In order to do this, they are sometimes required to provide copies of their cases, from which the board certifiers choose cases for the physician to present as part of the examination. The physician may then have to provide copies of patient records as part of this process.

The HIPAA Privacy Rule specifically allows protected health information to be used for certification activities as part of healthcare operations. The Privacy Rule allows a disclosure to be made from a covered entity, such as a hospital, to another treatment provider, such as a physician, for the physician's certification.

Physicians, in turn, can disclose the information to the specialty certification board for their own certifications as part of healthcare operations. However, in order for a covered entity physician to provide this information to an external entity, one of several alternatives must be met. First, the certification board could be a business associate (BA) and sign a BA agreement. Some certification boards have determined this is an appropriate solution to allow the information to be disclosed. Alternatively, if the information can be partially de-identified, for example, if the information is required to retain dates of procedure, but otherwise can be de-identified, then the physician needs a data use agreement with the certification board in order to provide a limited data set. If it is acceptable to the certification board, the records can be totally de-identified, which then means the protections of the Privacy Rule no longer apply to the information.

If none of these solutions work, the physician can obtain authorizations from the patients involved in the cases to allow the disclosure to the certification board.

References

Department of Health and Human Services. 45 CFR §§164.501, 164.506, 164.514.

Scenario 94

Can we share patient information with charitable organizations or disease-related foundations?

Alcohol and substance abuse laws

Federal Drug and Alcohol Treatment Program Regulations do not permit the disclosure of identifiable patient information unless the patient has signed an authorization.

The HIPAA Privacy Rule allows a covered entity to use protected health information for a broad range of activities necessary for the covered entity to stay in business. These activities include fundraising activities. Not only can a covered entity use limited protected health information for fundraising, but it can also disclose this information for fundraising to business associates hired for this purpose or to institutionally-related foundations.

An institutionally-related foundation has a specific meaning in the Privacy Rule. It is a foundation that qualifies as a nonprofit charitable foundation under section 501(c)(3) of the Internal Revenue Code. The foundation must also state in its charter statement of charitable purposes that it is formed to assist in fundraising of the covered entity.

An institutionally-related foundation does not include an organization that is formed for a more general charitable purpose, such as to support research about a specific disease, or to provide treatment for certain diseases. These types of foundations, even though they may contribute to the covered entity, are not formed for that purpose. Therefore, protected health information may not be disclosed to a foundation that is not institutionally related to the covered entity, unless the patient signs an authorization to do so.

References

Department of Health and Human Services. 45 CFR §§ 164.5014(f); 42 CFR § 2.12; Department of Health and Human Services. 2000. Final Rule: Standards for the Privacy of Individually Identifiable Health Information. *Federal Register* 65(250):82547.

Scenario 95

Is it okay for a facility's chaplain to call on patients?

Alcohol and substance abuse laws

Federal Drug and Alcohol Treatment Program Regulations permit the disclosure of information to Program workforce for treatment of the individual.

The HIPAA Privacy Rule allows a covered entity to use or disclose information for treatment of individuals. One of these treatment activities is to provide spiritual and cultural services to patients and their families.

The Privacy Rule allows for external clergy to find out names and locations of patients of their denomination in a facility, for patients willing to disclose their denominational preference. If a patient opts out of a facility directory, a clergyperson cannot obtain information about the patient's location, unless the patient or family gives the location directly to the clergyperson.

The rules for chaplains or pastoral care departments in a covered entity and those that apply to external clergy are different in the Privacy Rule. A chaplain or pastoral care provider is considered part of the workforce of the covered entity. These individuals must have training on the covered entity's privacy and security policies and procedures and are subject to the same sanctions as any other member of the covered entity's workforce should they not follow these policies or procedures. A chaplain should be able to access protected health information that is necessary for the chaplain's assigned role in the organization. A chaplain should have access to information on all patients being treated in the facility, including a patient who may have chosen to opt out of a facility directory.

Chaplains who also serve as clergy for external faith groups, however, must not use their access to the covered entity's protected health information when they have assumed their role as external clergy.

Chaplains or pastoral care departments often function as liaisons to the external religious community. They can assist the covered entity by providing education to external clergy regarding how the Privacy Rule works. They can often verify the identity of external clergy, if a facility decides that name badges for external clergy are required as part of visitor control.

References

Department of Health and Human Services. 45 CFR §§ 160.103, 164.501, 164.502, 164.514(d), 164.510; 42 CFR§ 2.12(b)(3).

Scenario 96

Is it okay to give access to patient information to a union representative to resolve a grievance?

 State and federal labor and worker's compensation laws

KEY WORDS TO SEARCH: grievance, representative

Alcohol and substance abuse laws

Federal Drug and Alcohol Treatment Program Regulations permit the disclosure of information to an entity having direct administrative control over that program. However, redisclosure of identifiable patient information to a person outside the Program is generally not permitted unless the patient has signed a consent or authorization. Consult legal counsel if there is an apparent conflict between the Program regulations and other state or federal laws or regulations.

The HIPAA Privacy Rule allows a covered entity to use protected health information for a broad range of activities that are considered healthcare operations. One of these activities is a resolution of internal grievances. If employees need to produce protected health information to prove that their employer is not accurate in an allegation that they provided poor care, for example, then employees are allowed to involve their employee representatives. Employee representatives may be union representatives. Further, under the National Labor Relations Act, the law may require the disclosure to an employee representative.

The minimum necessary requirements apply to this situation. An ideal would be if the information could be de-identified, or at least obvious identifiers removed, prior to the disclosure to the employee representative.

References

Department of Health and Human Services. 45 CFR §§ 164.501, 164.502(b); 42 CFR § 2.12. Department of Health and Human Services. 2000. Final Rule: Standards for the Privacy of Individually Identifiable Health Information. *Federal Register* 65(250):82492, 82599.

Scenario 97

Do we need a business associate agreement with an ambulance company?

United States Code considers ambulance services treatment; therefore, ambulance service companies are considered healthcare providers. Some nonfacility-based ambulance companies are covered entities, while others are not. It depends on whether their reimbursement involves one or more of the HIPAA-covered transactions. An example of a noncovered ambulance service may be one that is paid for by county taxes.

The HIPAA Privacy Rule states that business associate standards do not apply to disclosures made by one covered entity to another healthcare provider concerning the treatment of an individual. A business associate, on the other hand, is defined as a person who is not a member of a covered entity's workforce but performs certain functions on behalf of a covered entity. These functions do not include treatment of individuals. Therefore, a business associate agreement is not necessary with an ambulance service company.

The sharing of protected health information between treatment providers is not limited to the minimum necessary when treatment is involved; therefore, the covered facility does not need to be concerned with limiting the information available to the ambulance service when the service is transporting and treating a patient. The covered facility does, however, need to limit the information to the minimum necessary protected health information for the ambulance service's payment or healthcare operations purposes.

Finally, if a covered facility is concerned with how well an ambulance service is protecting the privacy of the individual's information while transporting the individual, it is important to remember that, if the ambulance company is a covered entity, it has an obligation to meet the standards of the Privacy Rule as well. If it is not, state record or licensure laws regarding privacy may govern the service. A covered entity is responsible for its own actions and violations of the Privacy Rule; it is not going to be held responsible for another independent agency's actions.

References

Department of Health and Human Services. 45 CFR §§ 160.402, 160.103, 164.502(e)(1), 164.514(d); United States Code 1395x(u) and 42 U.S.C. 1395x(s).

Scenario 98

We have a joint case review with all providers involved in the care of trauma patients. Can we share patient information in this forum, which includes emergency medical technicians (EMTs) and other providers?

 State and federal laws

KEY WORDS TO SEARCH: emergency medical services, trauma, and quality improvement

Ambulance services are considered treatment by United States Code. Therefore, ambulance service companies and their employed emergency medical technicians (EMTs), who provide emergency service treatment, are considered healthcare providers. Some nonfacility-based ambulance and emergency service providers are covered entities, whereas others are not; it depends on whether their reimbursement involves one or more of the HIPAA-covered transactions. An example of a noncovered ambulance service may be one that is paid for by county taxes, such as a fire department emergency response team.

The HIPAA Privacy Rule allows the sharing of minimum necessary information for improving the quality of healthcare. This is considered a part of healthcare operations. These disclosures for the assessment and outcomes of care can be made to other treatment providers as well, but only if the other treatment providers are covered entities. Otherwise, an authorization from the individual would be required before the case could be discussed with a noncovered entity.

In recognition of the fact that some emergency medicine treatment providers are not covered entities, some state public health laws have been enacted that require the disclosure in order to improve the quality of emergency treatment provided to its citizens.

If the disclosure is permitted either by the Privacy Rule or state law, emergency treatment providers should only be allowed to participate in the review of the individuals' cases for which they provided service, if the case review includes identifiable information. Some facilities schedule meetings so that all cases for one emergency treatment provider are reviewed together, after which the EMT provider is excused, and the next emergency treatment provider is invited in for case review.

References

Department of Health and Human Services. 45 CFR §§ 160.103, 164.501, 164.502(e)(1), 164.506(c), 164.512(a-b). United States Code 1395x(u) and 42 U.S.C. 1395x(s).

Scenario 99

May we share a mother's information with a collection agency, or other persons, when the mother asked to be anonymous because she put the baby up for adoption?

 State and federal laws

KEY WORDS TO SEARCH: consent, authorization, collection, fair debt collection practices, redaction, and adoption

The HIPAA Privacy Rule allows a covered entity to use protected health information for payment activities of the covered entity. Included in the definition of payment are collection activities. The covered entity needs to have a business associate agreement with any collection agency that undertakes these activities on behalf of the covered entity in order to allow the sharing of protected health information for this purpose. Also, the information shared is limited to the minimum necessary information for the collection of the debt.

One consideration in this scenario, however, is whether the covered entity agreed to the mother's request to be anonymous in regard to the payment of her claim. Any individual may request such a restriction, but the covered entity is not required to agree to it. A covered entity may agree to any restriction related to treatment, payment, or healthcare operations use of an individual's information, as well as to restrict information that otherwise could be given to family or friends involved in the individual's care. If the covered entity agrees to this restriction, it is required by the Privacy Rule to honor it, so the covered entity should be very careful in agreeing to restrictions. For example, if this mother was known to several members of the staff, the covered entity could agree to restrict access to the mother's records from those staff members, except in an emergency. However, it may be extremely difficult, if not impossible, for the covered entity to guarantee such a restriction. Most electronic health records do not have the capability to selectively restrict access to certain individuals, and, once agreed to, such a restriction to access the mother's records by these individuals would have to apply permanently, unless the mother terminates the restriction.

In order to remain anonymous from public inquiries, the mother should opt out of the facility directory.

Finally, state law, court directives, or facility policy govern the disclosure of a mother's name as part of the baby's records when an adoption occurs. Generally, if copies of records are provided to adopting parents, rather than a summary of the baby's birth records, a covered entity will redact or edit the mother's name, because she was promised confidentiality. This redaction is permitted as a nonreviewable denial of access to the personal representative of the baby.

References

Department of Health and Human Services. 45 CFR §§ 164.501, 164.510(a), 164.522(a), 164.524(a)(2)(v).

Scenario 100

May we share the most current minimum data set with a long-term care insurance provider without an authorization?

The HIPAA Privacy Rule includes long-term care insurers as covered health plans, except for issuers of fixed indemnity policies. A fixed indemnity or "per diem" policy pays up to a fixed benefit amount, regardless of the patient's costs for the care and, therefore, would not be engaging in HIPAA-covered transactions. If the issuer of the long-term fixed indemnity policy is not a covered entity, an authorization from the patient or the patient's personal representative would be required before disclosure of the patient's information. The issuer should provide a statement that they are or are not a covered health plan under the Privacy Rule.

A covered healthcare provider is permitted to disclose information to a covered health plan for the purpose of payment. The information from a minimum data set (MDS), usually the information that is pertinent to the patient's ability to perform activities of daily living, may be provided to the long-term care issuer in order to determine if the patient still qualifies for payments. However, the long-term care insurer should only be requesting the minimum necessary for this purpose, and the healthcare provider should only provide the information necessary for the payment purpose. The treatment provider can rely on the long-term care insurer, as another covered entity, to request only what is needed for the payment purpose and does not have to make the determination themselves.

In some cases, the healthcare provider may not be receiving the payment directly from the long-term care provider, or the healthcare provider may not be providing the long-term care. If the covered healthcare provider is not able to confirm the patient's coverage or that the individual is receiving long-term care services, an authorization may be requested from the long-term care insurer in order to demonstrate these facts to the healthcare provider.

References

Department of Health and Human Services. 45 CFR §§160.103, 164.501, 164.502; Department of Health and Human Services. 2000. Final Rule: Standards for the Privacy of Individually Identifiable Health Information. *Federal Register* 65(250): 82520 and Commentary CR15; Your Frequently Asked Questions On Privacy. 216. Available online from http://www.dhhs.gov/ocr/hipaa/.

Glossary of Long-Term Care. Available online from www.toddltc.com/NeedToKnow/Glossary.aspx#IndemnityPolicy/.

Scenario 101

Does HIPAA permit the individual's treatment records to automatically be sent to the patient's physician?

 State and federal laws

KEY WORDS TO SEARCH: consent, authorization

The practice of providing copies of an individual's treatment information to an individual's primary care provider, when another provider provides treatment, predates the HIPAA Privacy Rule. A similar practice occurs when a physician who is treating the patient in a facility will direct that a copy of the dictation be provided to the individual's primary care provider. The main reason for the so-called "courtesy copy" is to ensure that the primary care provider has information needed to ensure the continuity of the individual's care. In complex healthcare environments, this is sometimes the only way a primary care physician can obtain information about the care for which they referred the individual. With new technology, this distribution is often provided through auto-facsimile transmissions. With an electronic record, the information may often be accessible to the primary care provider at any time.

The disclosures permitted by a covered entity for the purpose of treatment in the Privacy Rule are broad. Treatment means the provision of healthcare, as well as the coordination or management of the healthcare of the individual between one or more healthcare providers. Treatment also covers consultation between more than one healthcare provider about the patient, or referrals of a patient for healthcare to another provider. Treatment disclosures such as "courtesy copies" should therefore be permitted by the Privacy Rule as a means of communication about the individual's treatment between more than one healthcare provider.

The concern about this automatic communication is that neither the individual nor the primary care physician initiates the communication. Sometimes, too, the individual decides to terminate the treatment relationship with the physician so that such a disclosure would no longer be for treatment. In that case, the individual does not believe the communication should continue. Or, individuals may decide they want a second opinion, for example, and want the second opinion information to be kept from their primary care physicians.

Not every disclosure for treatment implies that the individual requests it or that the healthcare provider initiates the contact. For example, the Privacy Rule permits the disclosure of information to a nursing home to assess placement, and even though the patient may not be aware of the communication or the nursing home requesting it, it is still considered a treatment disclosure.

It may be worthwhile for the covered entity to describe this activity in its Notice of Privacy Practices as one of the ways it uses and discloses information for treatment.

A covered entity can certainly ask the individual when the patient registers if his or her information on the patient's primary care physician is still accurate and update the information, as necessary. However, to deny a physician currently involved in a patient's care access to treatment information would require a patient to ask for a restriction and the covered entity to grant the restriction.

References

Department of Health and Human Services. 45 CFR §§ 164.501, 164.506(c), 164.520, 164.522.

Scenario 102

Can an affiliated foundation have access to an inpatient census? Should an internal department charged with fundraising have access?

Alcohol and substance abuse laws

Federal Drug and Alcohol Treatment Program Regulations permit disclosure of patient identity without consent if the purpose is for the administration of the Program. Fundraising activities would probably not be considered part of these administrative functions, and would, therefore, require a patient's signed consent.

The HIPAA Privacy Rule allows a covered entity to use protected health information, without authorization from the individual, for fundraising as part of allowable activities for the business management of the covered entity. The covered entity, an institutionally-related foundation, or a business associate of the covered entity can perform fundraising.

However, the Privacy Rule sets the minimum necessary disclosure permitted in these cases. The Rule states that patient demographics and dates of care can be used or disclosed for fundraising purposes. The definition of demographics is not included in the Rule itself, but is commonly interpreted in accordance with recommendations in the commentary to the Privacy Rule, which states demographics in this context means the individual's name, address and other contact information, age, gender, and insurance status. It does not allow access to diagnosis or type of treatment for this purpose.

The writers of the Privacy Rule addressed fundraising activities as though all contacts occurred after the individual was discharged. In reality, there are many other activities that are undertaken by administrative departments, business associates, and affiliated foundations that perform fundraising. The fundraisers may wish to visit a donor in the facility or send gifts or flowers, for example. Although not strictly for fundraising, these activities may be important to build the relationship with the individual. In order to determine if a donor or family of a donor is present in a facility, many often ask for access to the facility census. To the extent that the census can be limited to demographic and dates of stay, this access may be permitted as healthcare operations.

References

Department of Health and Human Services. 45 CFR §§ 164.501, 164.514(f), 42 CFR § 2.12(c)(4). Final Rule: Standards for the Privacy of Individually Identifiable Health Information. *Federal Register* 65(250): 82515 CR 1. Most Commonly Asked Questions and the Health Insurance Portability and Accountability Act of 1196 (HIPAA) also Known as the Privacy Rule. American Association of Healthcare Philanthropy. Available online from www.ahp.org/government-relations/hipaa/faq-on-hipaa.php.

Scenario 103

May we allow our facility attorney to review a patient's records in a possible litigation case?

Alcohol and substance abuse laws

Federal Drug and Alcohol Treatment Program Regulations permit the disclosure of information to an entity having direct administrative control over that program. However, it appears that these types of disclosures are limited to those necessary to provide the drug or alcohol treatment service; therefore, allowing an in-house attorney to review records because the patient may bring a lawsuit may not be permitted unless an authorization from the patient is obtained.

The HIPAA Privacy Rule allows a covered entity to disclose protected health information for the healthcare operations of the covered entity without a specific consent or authorization from the patient. One of the healthcare operations mentioned in the Privacy Rule is conducting or arranging for legal services.

This disclosure must be limited, however, to the minimum necessary protected health information for the purpose; the covered entity can trust its attorney to only ask for the information needed. The other condition that applies is: the reason the attorney is reviewing the case must be related to the covered entity's permitted use under the Privacy Rule. For example, if a patient is thinking of suing because of the treatment he or she received from the facility, it is permitted for the facility's attorney to review the related records. It would not be permitted, however, for the facility's attorney to review the protected health information of an employee of the facility because the employee is bringing an employment discrimination lawsuit against the facility.

Finally, as with other healthcare operations, these services can be provided by an attorney who is a member of the workforce or an outside attorney with whom the facility has a business associate agreement.

References

Department of Health and Human Services. 45 CFR §§164.501, 164.506; Department of Health and Human Services, Office for Civil Rights. Your Frequently Asked Questions On Privacy. 710. Available online from http://www.dhhs.gov/ocr/hipaa/.

Department of Health and Human Services. 42 CFR § 2.12(c)(3).

Scenario 104

Can a workers' compensation carrier obtain all the past records of an injured employee?

State and federal laws

KEY WORDS TO SEARCH: labor commission, workers' compensation

State and federal labor and worker's compensation laws
Federal laws and regulations relating to workers' compensation: Black Lung Benefits Act, the federal Employees' Compensation Act, the Longshore and Harbor Workers' Compensation Act, and the Energy Employees' Occupational Illness Compensation Program Act

Alcohol and substance abuse laws
Federal Drug and Alcohol Treatment Program Record Regulations require any patient receiving Program services to sign a consent or authorization prior to access or disclosure of information identifying the patient as receiving these treatment services.

The healthcare provider may disclose past records based on workers' compensation laws or regulations (either state or federal) that apply to the injured or ill worker if these laws and regulations permit the workers' compensation carrier to obtain this information without additional authorizations by the worker. This disclosure can be made to a workers' compensation carrier or to a party responsible for payment of workers' compensation benefits to the individual and to an agency responsible for administering and/or adjudicating the individual's claim for workers' compensation benefits.

Workers' compensation carriers are not under the purview of the HIPAA Privacy Rule, and because there is so much variation in state and federal workers' compensation rules, the Privacy Rule defaults to whatever law or regulation applies, rather than disrupt the benefits to the worker.

However, unless the workers' compensation law states otherwise, the minimum necessary standard applies to these disclosures. The workers' compensation carrier should only be requesting the information needed to pay for the care, determine extent of disability, or determine if there is a pre-existing condition.

References

Department of Health and Human Services. 45 CFR § 164.512(l); Department of Health and Human Services. 2000. Final Rule: Standards for the Privacy of Individually Identifiable Health Information. *Federal Register* 65(250): 82543.

Scenario 105

Are we required to send a lifetime's worth of records to a health plan if they make it a condition of paying a claim?

 State and federal laws

KEY WORDS TO SEARCH: HIV, AIDS, sexually transmitted disease, mental health, psychological, psychiatric, genetic test, and consent

 Alcohol and substance abuse laws

Federal Drug and Alcohol Treatment Program Record Regulations require any patient receiving Program services to sign a consent or authorization prior to access or disclosure of information identifying the patient as receiving these treatment services.

Unless more stringent state or federal record protections apply requiring specific patient consent or authorization for payment, the HIPAA Privacy Rule allows a healthcare provider to disclose protected health information (PHI) for payment purposes without a specific consent or authorization from the patient.

A health plan needs the PHI for two main purposes: to justify the payment of a specific claim or to determine whether the health plan is responsible for the coverage on the specific claim. The latter determination is often made by reviewing the records to see if a pre-existing condition exists that would negate the payer's obligation to pay the claim. The request for a "lifetime" of records is usually for the purpose of determining a pre-existing condition.

The health plan is a covered entity under the Privacy Rule. The plan has an obligation to request the minimum necessary for the purpose. The request for a "lifetime" of records would appear to be in violation of this minimum necessary standard.

The healthcare provider, in responding to this request, must also disclose the minimum necessary amount of PHI. Because the healthcare provider does not know what pre-existing conditions the payer is looking for, the healthcare provider may disclose the records obviously related to the claim, along with a response to the health plan that its request exceeds the minimum necessary standard. Normally, a covered entity can rely on another covered entity to only request the minimum necessary for its purpose, as the minimum necessary standard applies to both covered entities. However, the disclosing entity does have the right to challenge the requesting entity and to negotiate an information exchange that satisfies both parties. When the dispute cannot be resolved, the patient should also be informed, in case the health plan denies the claim; the patient can then dispute the issue with the health plan or decide to sign an authorization for the disclosure.

References

Department of Health and Human Services. 45 CFR §§164.501, 164.502(a)(1)(ii), 164.502(b)(1); Department of Health and Human Services. 42 CFR§ 2.13. Your Frequently Asked Questions On Privacy. 216. Available online from http://www.dhhs.gov/ocr/hipaa/.

Scenario 106

Does the HIPAA Privacy Rule require us to protect HIV or AIDS patients' records from access within the covered entity?

 ### State and federal laws

KEY WORDS TO SEARCH: HIV, AIDS, sexually transmitted disease, and genetic test

 ### Alcohol and substance abuse laws

Federal Drug and Alcohol Treatment Program Record Regulations require any patient receiving Program services to sign a consent or authorization prior to access or disclosure of information identifying the patient as receiving these treatment services. This applies even to a treatment provider outside the Program, except in a bona fide medical emergency or other very limited circumstances.

The Privacy Rule does not restrict access to records based on diagnosis. The only type of record to which it applies restrictions is a psychotherapy note. The Rule also recognizes that the patient has a right to request restrictions on records, as long as the covered entity has agreed to the restriction.

There are laws in many states, however, that are often more protective of certain types of records, such as for those patients who have HIV or AIDS. Often, too, these laws restrict the disclosure of this information outside the covered entity unless the patient has signed very specific authorizations.

There are also state laws that prevent certain types of entities from requesting or acting on such diagnoses. For example, a health plan may be restricted from requesting HIV or AIDS or genetic test result information because the plan may use the information to cancel the coverage for that patient.

References

Department of Health and Human Services. 45 CFR §§164.501, 164.508(a)(2); Department of Health and Human Services. 42 CFR§§ 2.13, 2.31, 2.51.

SECTION VII

Sanctions and Compliance

This section discusses ways to monitor compliance with the Privacy Rule, dealing with complaints and actions against those in the workforce when they do not comply with a covered entities' privacy policies. Reporting breaches of privacy and mitigation to individuals is also addressed.

Scenario 107

How can we monitor compliance with verbal permission situations?

One of the requirements of the HIPAA Privacy Rule is that verbal permission of individuals be obtained in certain situations prior to the disclosure of their protected health information. The permission to be listed in a facility directory is one of these situations. It is fairly easy to monitor compliance with the individual's request by reviewing the facility directory's listing and verifying the preference with the individual, when necessary. Another good way to monitor compliance is by reviewing complaints. If an individual wants privacy enough to express this preference, the individual will often complain when his or her preference is not met.

The other common type of situation occurs when verbal permission of the individual should be sought before discussing information with friends or relatives. Monitoring compliance in this situation is more difficult.

One way of monitoring compliance is to first have clinical departments develop protocols for dealing with the situation, such as always having unknown visitors step out of the room in order to make the individual comfortable with expressing his or her decision. Once such a protocol is developed, clinical staff should be trained in following the protocol.

Peer monitoring, periodic reminders of what the protocol states, or even posters to raise awareness can reinforce compliance. A manager can observe employee practices. Finally, the privacy office or patient relations department can monitor complaints to see if there should be more training provided in certain clinical areas or for certain employees.

References

Department of Health and Human Services, 45 CFR §§164.510, 164.530(b) and (d).

Scenario 108

What should we do if we identify a breach of privacy in our electronic health record by the employee of an external provider?

State and federal laws

KEY WORDS TO SEARCH: identity theft, electronic breach reporting, mitigation of breaches, and qualified service agreement (QSA)

Alcohol and substance abuse laws

Federal Drug and Alcohol Treatment Program Regulations require a signed authorization from a patient before any disclosure can be made, even for treatment, except in emergency situations. Allowing a provider and staff outside the Program to have access, although extremely risky, might be arranged if there was a qualified service agreement in place with the provider. If a breach could be proved in that situation, the provider would be in violation of the qualified service agreement. Violations may be reported to a United States District Attorney in the location of the violation.

As a covered entity with an electronic medical record extends electronic access to protected health information to affiliated providers and their staffs, it is important to establish user agreements between the two parties that address what happens when a breach is suspected or confirmed. These agreements should state the expectation that a provider will follow established sanctions when a breach is identified by the provider of the electronic record. This agreement should also discuss possible consequences to the provider as the result of inappropriate activities by staff, lack of action by the provider, or multiple violations occurring at once. The actions described could include termination of access to an individual provider or provider's staff member or termination of user access to the electronic system for all of the provider's staff.

The covered entity with the electronic medical record may not have authority over the staff of the provider, but the provider is often a covered entity under the HIPAA Privacy Rule. As such, the provider must meet the provisions of the Privacy Rule, including sanctions of workforce and possible mitigation of breaches.

On the other hand, the provider of the electronic medical record has responsibilities to safeguard the protected health information it maintains, as well as additional requirements under the HIPAA Security Rule. A covered entity who provides an electronic record must ensure appropriate access controls, auditing of access, and logging a response to security incidents.

If a breach by a staff member of another covered entity occurs, it is possible that both covered entities will be held accountable under different sections of the Privacy and Security Rules if their responses to the incident are not appropriate.

References

Department of Health and Human Services. 45 CFR §§ 164.530 (c), (e), (f), 160.402, 160.306(b), 164.308, 164.312; 42 CFR §§ 2.2, 2.4–5.

Scenario 109

How often should we update privacy policies and procedures or audit our compliance?

 State and federal laws

KEY WORDS TO SEARCH: changes in privacy, security, required reporting, identity theft, and breach reporting

The HIPAA Privacy Rule does not define how often polices or procedures should be reviewed or changed, except to indicate the changes must be done, as necessary, to comply with changes in laws. Other requirements may dictate the timing of policy reviews, such as when a covered entity is also accredited by The Joint Commission. The Joint Commission usually requires all policies to be reviewed every three years. Other triggers to review and update policies may be changes in the mission of the organization, changes in the desired practices, or changes in senior management.

Best practices often suggest conducting a privacy walk-through several times a year, in order to spot check visible evidence of compliance with the Privacy Rule, such as Notice of Privacy Practices posters in admitting areas. Areas that have been identified as high risk for incidental disclosures should probably be included in a walk-through as well, to determine if workforce is making reasonable efforts to keep such disclosures at a minimum.

Risk assessments are usually performed initially to determine potential risks to privacy or security for systems or records that contain protected health information. If a risk assessment is done and any risks addressed or mitigated, there is no need to conduct another unless there have been changes in the procedures, systems, or environment.

However, areas at higher risk for noncompliance may be identified either through a risk assessment or through monitoring of privacy complaints. A focused audit may be done, as needed, when an individual privacy complaint or issue suggests workforce may not be compliant with existing policies or procedures. An annual review of all privacy-related complaints could be used to trend issues and identify areas of concern.

A procedure may be a good candidate for a focused compliance audit when it involves a particularly complex area of the regulation, or when there is high turnover of workforce. A sample of authorizations can be reviewed to ensure that the authorizations meet the requirements of the Privacy Rule and to verify that the requested information was sent. Also, an audit may be done to ensure that requests by individuals for their own information were processed within the time required by the Privacy Rule. It is a good practice to perform one of these types of focused audits at least quarterly.

Finally, certain audits may need to be done daily. If a high profile patient is currently in a facility, as an example, access logs may need to be checked daily to determine whether the access by workforce is appropriate.

References

Department of Health and Human Services. 45 CFR §164.530(i)(2).

Scenario 110

Can individuals be charged under the criminal penalties of HIPAA, or only covered entities?

The HIPAA Privacy Rule applies to covered entities. Covered entities are health plans, healthcare clearinghouses, healthcare providers who transmit health information in covered transactions, and Medicare prescription drug card sponsors.

The Department of Justice has jurisdiction over the criminal penalties and prosecutions, whereas the Office for Civil Rights has jurisdiction over civil penalties and actions in the HIPAA Privacy Rule.

A Department of Justice memorandum was distributed in June 2005, in which the General Counsel for the Department of Health and Human Services and the Senior Counsel to the Deputy Attorney General provided a legal opinion on the subject of how the criminal enforcement provisions of HIPAA could be applied. Their conclusions were that: First, a covered entity is liable for prosecution under HIPAA. Second, certain directors, officers, and employees of covered entities may be liable for prosecution, in accordance with general principles of corporate criminal liability, especially if it can be proved that the employee was acting to benefit the covered entity.

Finally, a person outside the covered entity may or may not be liable for prosecution or penalties. Much depends on whether the person "knows" that the activity was contrary to statute or regulation, or whether the person can be prosecuted for aiding and abetting the crime.

The criminal prosecutions of violations of the HIPAA Privacy Rule, to this point, have been of individuals, not covered entities. Each of these individuals has been an employee of a covered entity and used protected health information that he or she obtained from his or her employment for personal gain.

It will be cases such as these, when decided in court, that will finally answer this question.

References

Department of Health and Human Services. 42 U.S.C § 1230d-6(200); 45 CFR §§ 160.103, 160.402. Azar, Alex M. and Coleman, Timothy J. 2005. Memorandum: Scope of Criminal Enforcement Under 42 U.S.C § 1320d-6. Available online from www.worldprivacyforum.org/pdf/hipaa_opinion_06_01_2005.pdf

Scenario 111

A patient has a privacy complaint about another covered entity. What should we recommend to the patient?

A covered entity is required by the HIPAA Privacy Rule to create a process to handle complaints from individuals who feel their privacy rights have been violated by the covered entity, or when individuals feel the covered entity has not protected their information as required by the Privacy Rule. In addition, the covered entity needs to have designated a contact person for the organization to handle complaints, usually the privacy officer. Finally, a covered entity cannot discriminate or initiate any reprisals against individuals for exercising their rights allowed by the Privacy Rule, or for complaining about the covered entity's actions.

A patient should be encouraged to first complain to the covered entity whose actions generated the complaint. If the covered entity is required to have a Notice of Privacy Practices, such a notice should contain specific information about how to contact the privacy officer or office to file a complaint. A patient should be able to request a copy of the Notice of Privacy Practices from the covered entity.

If the patient is not satisfied with the covered entity's response, or does not wish to contact the covered entity, the patient may complain directly to the Office for Civil Rights. When filing a complaint with the Office for Civil Rights, the complaint:

♦ Must be filed in writing, either on paper or electronically

♦ Must name the entity that is the subject of the complaint and describe the acts or omissions believed to be in violation of the Privacy Rule, and

♦ Must be filed within 180 days of when the complainant knew, or should have known, that the act or omission complained of occurred, unless this time limit is waived by the Secretary.

Details about filing a complaint can be found on the Web site for the DHHS Office for Civil Rights at www.dhhs.gov/ocr/privacyhowtofile.htm.

References

Department of Health and Human Services. 45 CFR §§ 164.530 (a), (d), (g), 164.520(c), 160.306(b).

Scenario 112

Should we take action against a business associate for accidental disclosures?

 State and federal laws

KEY WORDS TO SEARCH: privacy breach notification requirements, identity theft

An accidental disclosure is not the same as an incidental disclosure. An incidental disclosure is an inadvertent disclosure made as a by-product of an otherwise permitted disclosure. An accidental disclosure, on the other hand, is a disclosure not permitted by the HIPAA Privacy Rule, but made because of error or neglect.

If a business associate makes an error and discloses information as a result, the business associate agreement requires that the disclosure be reported to the covered entity. The covered entity does not have an obligation to monitor the activities of a business associate, according to the Privacy Rule. However, if the business associate appears to have a pattern of making accidental disclosures, the covered entity does have the obligation to demand the business associate determine what is causing the problem and to fix it. The obligation falls on the covered entity ultimately to "cure the breach or violation." The business associate should demonstrate to the covered entity that it is taking reasonable steps to safeguard the protected health information.

If the business associate continues with the same problems, then the covered entity has a decision to make. The covered entity must decide if the activity of the business associate is resulting in a significant breach or major violation of the regulation that, as a consequence, is a breach of the business associate agreement. If so, the covered entity must terminate the contract and find another business associate to perform the service. If that is not possible, the covered entity must report the business associate to the Secretary of Health and Human Services.

The steps the Secretary may take after that are not yet clear, as the business associate is not a covered entity, and its obligation to meet the standards of the Privacy Rule is imposed by contract, not by the regulation. However, the covered entity, by terminating the contract or contacting the Secretary, has just minimized the risk of liability under HIPAA for any civil penalties that the Secretary might have imposed because of violations of the Privacy Rule.

References

Department of Health and Human Services. 45 CFR §§ 164.504; 160.402(c). Department of Health and Human Services. 2000. Final Rule: Standards for the Privacy of Individually Identifiable Health Information. *Federal Register* 65(250): 14786, 82562.

Scenario 113

A vendor has brought a marketing person to the facility, and he reviewed patient information. Is that a violation of HIPAA?

In some cases, the vendor is a treatment provider. For example, the vendor might be fitting a prosthetic device on a patient. However, vendors are rarely covered entities under the HIPAA Privacy Rule, because they do not bill using standard transactions. Also, unless the vendor is providing a service for the covered entity, such as software support, the covered entity does not usually have a business associate agreement with a vendor.

A vendor usually fits into the category of a "visitor." Visitors or other noncovered entities are not under the purviews of the Privacy Rule; therefore, they generally cannot violate the HIPAA Privacy Rule.

However, the covered entity could be in violation of HIPAA when a breach like this occurs, in that the covered entity has the obligation to safeguard protected health information from inappropriate disclosures. The covered entity may also have obligations dictated by the HIPAA Security Rule to control and validate individuals' access to a facility based on its role or function, and also to control visitor access to certain areas.

There are limited circumstances where a covered entity may give protected health information to a vendor. Protected health information may be given to vendors if they are involved in the treatment of an individual. Information also may be disclosed to a vendor if the vendor is working for a company that is subject to the jurisdiction of the Food and Drug Administration regarding its product or activity. Information that can be disclosed is that which is related to quality, safety or effectiveness of the product, and reported adverse events, product defects, and tracking of the product, as well as enabling the product to be recalled, or conducting of post-marketing surveillance. "Post-marketing surveillance" is not marketing; it is an activity related to determining the safety or effectiveness of a product after it has been approved and is in commercial distribution, as well as certain Phase IV (post-approval) commitments by pharmaceutical companies. Any other disclosure of protected health information to a vendor should only be an incidental disclosure.

Best practices for vendor relationships may be for the covered entity to require vendors to attend orientation classes, during which the expectations for behavior while in the facility are set. The orientation should cover what protected health information the covered entity is permitted to disclose to the vendor and what areas of the facility the vendors are allowed to visit. Vendors should be issued badges that clearly identify them to staff and patients. Finally, a process to sanction the vendor should be established, with the ultimate sanction of being banned from the facility.

References

Department of Health and Human Services. 45 CFR §§ 164.310, 164.512(b), 164.530(c); Department of Health and Human Services. 2000. Final Rule: Standards for the Privacy of Individually Identifiable Health Information. *Federal Register* 65(250): 82526.

Scenario 114

We had a disgruntled ex-employee who stole patient demographic information and is now using the information to call patients. What can we do?

State and federal laws

KEY WORDS TO SEARCH: privacy breach notification requirements, identity theft

Alcohol and substance abuse laws

Violations of the Federal Drug and Alcohol Treatment Program Regulations may be reported to a United States District Attorney in the location of the violation.

Contact your legal counsel immediately to determine the facility's options. Certain legal actions may be taken, such as obtaining a restraining order, or an order to cease and desist the activity.

Based on your legal counsel's recommendations, send a certified letter to the ex-employee stating that the facility's privacy policies are being violated, and that information used was accessed based on an assigned role with the facility to obtain protected health information for a purpose not allowed by the HIPAA Privacy Rule. Any further use of the protected health information may constitute a violation of the Privacy Rule. Point out that the criminal prosecutions of violations of the HIPAA Privacy Rule to this point have been of individuals, not covered entities. Each of these individuals has been an employee of a covered entity and used protected health information that he or she obtained from his or her employment for personal purposes. Further, include that these individuals were convicted and their sentences included both fines and jail terms.

If available, review the access logs for this person to determine if he or she abused his or her access rights by accessing records the individual should not have while an employee of the facility. Check to see whether other documents or files have been removed from the facility. All of these things can be used in possible legal actions against this former employee.

Also, if this person is a licensed professional, such activity on his or her part may be illegal or unethical, and their actions can be reported to the appropriate licensure board.

Inform your public relations department to ensure they are aware of the situation and can prepare appropriate responses if a patient or the media contacts them.

Consider other steps to prevent future incidents. Create and obtain confidentiality agreements from employees in which they agree to keep patient information confidential, even after they are no longer employed by the facility. Review facility privacy and security polices and processes to see if they can be improved. Would a structured review of access audit logs have identified the employee's activity as being unusual? Are employees' access logs routinely audited when employees leave employment? Is access to electronic systems terminated when an employee is terminated? Are training programs adequate to communicate privacy and security policies and procedures, and consequences of breaches? All of these actions may lessen the risk of similar incidents in the future.

References

Department of Health and Human Services. 45 CFR §§164.502, 164.308; 42 § CFR 2.5.

Scenario 115

Should we initiate sanctions against an employee based on a patient's complaint alone, without additional proof?

The HIPAA Privacy Rule states that a covered entity must receive and document complaints from individuals. In addition, the covered entity must have and apply appropriate sanctions against members of its workforce when they violate the standards or the privacy policies or procedures established by the covered entity.

Beyond that, the Privacy Rule does not state how much evidence is required to prove that a complaint is valid. An access audit log may be a valuable tool to prove or disprove access by an employee but cannot provide evidence of a subsequent redisclosure by the employee in violation of the Privacy Rule.

The best process is to objectively investigate the complaint. Interviews can be conducted with the accused employee, the employee's coworkers, or the employee's manager. Records of the patient may be reviewed for internal complaint resolution purposes to determine if the employee's access was based on an assigned role by the covered entity. If an employee has adequate training and a good track record of compliance with privacy policies and procedures, and there is no additional proof, there may be no reason to discipline the employee. Unfortunately, individuals may try to get an employee in trouble because of reasons outside of the workplace.

An employee has rights to privacy, too. The covered entity should decide what it may disclose to a complainant after an investigation has been conducted. Often, the complainant is only told that a breach was or was not confirmed, and that appropriate actions were taken. If the complainant does not feel the covered entity's response was adequate, the complainant has the option of filing a complaint with the Department of Health and Human Service's Office for Civil Rights.

References

Department of Health and Human Services. 45 CFR §§ 164.530, 163.306.

Scenario 116

Should we sanction an employee who disclosed patient information by mistake?

The HIPAA Privacy Rule requires that the covered entity apply appropriate sanctions against employees who fail to comply with the privacy policies and procedures of the covered entity. There is not a requirement that the covered entity impose certain sanctions, such as terminate the employee who fails to comply with the privacy policies or procedures. Also, an employee cannot be held accountable if another entity makes a mistake. For example, if an employee addressed the information to the correct address, but the post office did not deliver it to the right place, the employee should not be held accountable.

It is appropriate to sanction the employee if he or she did not comply with policies or procedures, but what sanction is appropriate? Most entities establish recommended sanctions based on several factors: Was the disclosure accidental or intentional? Was a procedure not followed, and, therefore, the employee was clearly negligent? Is there a risk of harm to the patient or to the organization? What was included in the information that was disclosed and to whom was it disclosed? What has been the employee's past performance? How adequate has his or her training been?

Note, too, that the sanctions are applied when the employee does not meet the covered entity's privacy policies and procedures, as opposed to when an employee violates the Privacy Rule. It is up to the covered entity to ensure that its privacy policies and procedures address the provisions of the Privacy Rule. Therefore, one of the steps in a case like this is to examine the policy and procedures that apply to the incident. Do they clearly explain what the Privacy Rule requires? Do they define steps that must be taken to reduce the likelihood of an accidental disclosure? If the mistake is due to duplicate names, for example, is there an adequate tool in place to highlight duplications, to ensure that the wrong person's information is not sent in the future?

There is also the matter of consistency in sanctions. What was done in the organization in the past for similar incidents? If the facility does not have a history of this type of incident, what precedent for the situation should be set should it happen again?

Finally, the human resources department in the covered entity should be involved in the decision to sanction an employee, because it will be aware of other employment-related laws or union concerns that may apply to the situation.

References

Department of Health and Human Services. 45 CFR § 164.530(e)(1).

Scenario 117

What criteria should we use to identify inappropriate access when reviewing access audit logs?

 State and federal laws

KEY WORDS TO SEARCH: privacy breach notification requirements, identity theft, and electronic audit logs

It is a requirement of the HIPAA Security Rule to implement ways that document access to information systems that contain electronic protected health information. Included in the same standard is the requirement that covered entities examine the activity in these access audit logs.

Electronic audit logs generate a great deal of raw data, depending on how they are constructed in the software. Often they record every access to every data element or document type; time stamps that record when the person accessed the record, first opened the document, and when the document was closed; whether the person viewed, created, updated, or deleted the information; the user's id, the owner of the record; and the physical location on the network where the access occurred. Multiply this documentation by the number of times the caregivers legitimately accessed records of a particular patient daily, and it gives an idea of the degree of data accumulated daily in these audit logs.

That is why it is important to structure a process to review the data. Some covered entities focus on high profile patients, such as athletes, actors, public officials, physicians, employees, well-known persons in the community, individuals mentioned in the news, or patients with certain diagnoses. Those who conduct high profile patient audits often identify the patients by reviewing newspaper accounts or by asking their administration to inform them when a high profile patient has been admitted.

Other algorithms have been successfully used by covered entities for routine identification of possible inappropriate access by users. Of course, use of the algorithm depends on the amount of information available in the audit logs, and whether links to the user's files are possible. The auditor looks for a match with the user's last name and patient's last name; user's work location and patient's work location; and the nine-digit zip code of the user matching the nine-digit zip code of the patient. Once these possible inappropriate accesses are identified, further investigation is required to confirm whether a breach occurred.

References

Department of Health and Human Services. 45 CFR §164.312.

Scenario 118

Do we have to inform the patient when we sanction an employee for breaching his or her privacy?

 State and federal laws

KEY WORDS TO SEARCH: identity theft, electronic breach reporting, employee or worker rights

There is no requirement in the HIPAA Privacy Rule that a patient be informed of the sanctions applied to an employee of a covered entity. If an inappropriate disclosure was made by an employee, some information can be included in an accounting of disclosures should the patient ask for one; but this accounting is not required to include the details of the person who made the disclosure.

For good customer service and to reduce the number of complaints filed with the Office for Civil Rights, when a patient files a complaint, it is a good practice to acknowledge the complaint and thank the patient for bringing it to the covered entity's attention. After the investigation has been completed, a response informing the patient that the investigation has been completed and results of the investigation should be sent. The amount of detail in the response may depend on the situation.

If no breach was found, the letter needs to demonstrate that the investigation was thorough and that the covered entity is not concealing the incident.

If a breach is confirmed, human resources and legal counsel may need to be consulted to provide input about the degree of information that should be included in the response. Suggested content could state that the investigation found a problem and that the covered entity should apologize to the patient and affirm its commitment to protecting privacy. The response should indicate that appropriate sanctions were applied to any employees involved, or if there was a process problem identified, that the problem was addressed. Information on how and with whom to follow up should also be provided to the patient, in case he or she identifies any ramifications from the breach.

Detailed information that would compromise the security of the covered entity or that might jeopardize discipline or legal action against employees or others involved in a breach should not be included. Many covered entities do not disclose the identity of the employee responsible for the breach for this reason. There may be union rules that apply to the discipline requiring confidentiality for the employee. Also, the covered entity may be required by state laws to keep the information about disciplinary actions against employees confidential. If the patient has already named a specific employee he or she believes is responsible for the breach, it may be necessary to confirm the allegations, if true, or deny them if the investigation could not prove the employee was responsible.

If mitigation is appropriate, include this in the response. Depending on the nature of the breach, there may also be state or federal laws that require certain information be provided to the patient whose privacy was breached.

References

Department of Health and Human Services. 45 CFR §164.528.

SECTION VIII

Special Use and Disclosure Situations

This section deals with a variety of situations in which special rules may apply to disclosures of patient information from a covered entity. Poison control centers, health oversight agencies, research projects, and dealings with the media are some examples of the scenarios discussed in this section.

Scenario 119

Is it okay to give information to a cancer registry?

 State and federal laws

KEY WORDS TO SEARCH: public health reporting of cancer cases

Cancer registries are created for multiple purposes. They can be used to provide population-based studies to determine outcomes of treatment for a covered entity. The establishment and maintenance of a cancer registry is often a requirement of certain types of accreditation. These registries often feed into larger, regional databases and are used for public health-related trending. The cancer registry data is often used for research, as well.

Many states require that information be reported to cancer registries in order to allow the data to be used for public health purposes. In that case, the covered entity can consider the disclosure as permitted by the HIPAA Privacy Rule because it is required reporting for public health purposes.

When disclosure is not required by law, a covered entity may disclose information to another covered entity's cancer registry for the purpose of outcomes evaluation and development of clinical guidelines. This is permitted in the Privacy Rule, even when the healthcare operation is actually for the other covered entity. When disclosing protected health information to another covered entity for the other's healthcare operations, certain conditions must be met. The first condition is that the patient needs to have received services from both entities.

The second condition is that the reason for the disclosure must fall within a subset of healthcare operations as defined in the Privacy Rule. Treatment outcomes evaluation and clinical guideline development are two reasons included in this healthcare operations subset.

The third condition is that the information disclosed should be the minimum necessary for the purpose. Disclosing current patient condition and contact information to the other covered entity would meet the minimum necessary condition. Therefore, a physician's clinic may provide patient follow-up information to the cancer registry of a facility for the evaluation of cancer treatment provided by the facility.

Once the information is included in a covered entity's cancer registry, it is still under the protections of the Privacy Rule, even though it is probably not a designated record set. Cancer registry data is generally not used to make any decisions about the care of an individual patient; it is used in the aggregate for other purposes. Reports from the cancer registry can be disclosed for public health purposes as permitted by law. The covered entity may use the information to determine outcomes and develop clinical protocols as part of healthcare operations. Research can be performed using the information when approved by an Institutional Review Board or a Privacy Board.

References

Department of Health and Human Services. 45 CFR §§ 164.506, 164.512.

Scenario 120

Do all research projects require records to be de-identified?

State and federal laws, Common Rule and FDA regulations

KEY WORDS TO SEARCH: research, HIV/HIV mental health, and genetic test results

Alcohol and substance abuse laws

Federal Drug and Alcohol Treatment Program Regulations do permit disclosures to researchers without patient consent. The HIPAA Privacy Rule provisions on research must also be followed if the Program is a covered entity. Also, the researcher is strictly prohibited from redisclosing identifying information except back to the Program. Also, no identifying information the researcher obtains can be used in a criminal investigation.

The research provisions in the HIPAA Privacy Rule allow several ways to conduct data collection in research. The Institutional Review Board (IRB) or a Privacy Board, in certain circumstances, has to authorize how the researcher is to proceed with data collection for the research project.

The Privacy Rule states that the data may be de-identified prior to the disclosure to the researcher. This de-identification can be done by the covered entity or carried out by a business associate. The researcher can also do the de-identification as a business associate. With paper records, this is a very onerous process. All 18 identifiers must be redacted from the record copy if the covered entity meets the safe harbor standards. With an electronic data extract, on the other hand, it is a fairly easy process.

A second option is to provide the researcher a limited data set. This still is onerous when used with paper records, but the covered entity can leave dates and zip code information in the copies. When using an electronic data download, once again, it is much easier to produce a limited data set. And, again, a business associate may create a limited data set. The researcher must sign a data use agreement before the limited data set can be disclosed.

Another option is for an IRB or Privacy Board to grant the researcher a waiver of authorization. If the researcher meets certain conditions, this waiver allows him or her access to identifiable information without patient authorization. In order for the researcher to obtain a waiver from the IRB Privacy Board, the Board must be satisfied that the research poses no more than a minimal risk to the privacy of the individuals, that it is not practical for the researcher to obtain authorizations from the research subjects, and that the researcher needs the access to the identifiable information for the project. In making the determination of minimal risk, the Board receives assurances from the researcher that any identifiers will be destroyed at the earliest opportunity, that the identifiable information will be adequately protected during the course of the project, and that no reuse or redisclosure of the identifiable information without appropriate approvals will occur. However, accounting of disclosure provisions apply when authorization waivers are granted.

When other conditions of the Privacy Rule are met, the researcher may also access fully-identifiable information for preparing a research protocol, or to do research on decedent patients' records.

Finally, if the researcher obtains a HIPAA-compliant authorization from the patient prior to the data collection, the researcher can have that information the patient permits the researcher to have.

References

Department of Health and Human Services. 45 CFR §§ 164.512(i), 164.514; 42 CFR § 2.52, 2.62. Subpart A of Title 45 CFR Part 46; Food and Drug Administration. Title 21 CFR Parts 50 and 56. Multiple documents on research and HIPAA available online from http://privacyruleandresearch.nih.gov/.

Scenario 121

Are research databases protected by HIPAA?

 State and federal laws, Common Rule and FDA regulations

KEY WORDS TO SEARCH: research, HIV/HIV, mental health, genetic test results, tissue bank, and specimen bank

 Alcohol and substance abuse laws
Federal Drug and Alcohol Treatment Program regulations do permit disclosures to researchers without patient consent. The HIPAA Privacy Rule provisions on research must also be followed, if the Program is a covered entity. Also, the researcher is strictly prohibited from redisclosing identifying information except back to the Program. Also, no identifying information the researcher obtains can be used in a criminal investigation.

A research database is under the protections of the HIPAA Privacy Rule only when certain conditions are met. First, the database must have been created or maintained by a covered entity. Second, it must contain identifiable information.

To be considered identifiable, the database must contain at least one of the 18 identifiers found in the Privacy Rule, or some other data element, which used alone or in combination with other information in the database would allow the individual to be identified. Tissue or blood sample banks are considered de-identified if they do not have associated information that identifies the source of the sample.

It is possible to consider the database de-identified if all the identifiers are removed except for a unique code for each patient. The reason the covered entity may decide to do this is to allow the covered entity the option of re-identifying the data set in the future. However, a code for the patient must not be generated using an identifiable element; for example, patient initials or scrambled medical record numbers cannot be used to create these codes. Also, the covered entity must retain the key to re-identifying the patient and never disclose it to the researcher to use to re-identify the patients.

In order to create a research database, the researcher must obtain approval from an Institutional Review Board (or a Privacy Board in certain circumstances). The original data to create the database can be obtained by seeking an authorization from the patient, or by a waiver of authorization if the researcher meets certain criteria and the IRB approves the waiver.

Once a de-identified database is created, the Privacy Rule requirements for research do not have to be met for future projects done using this database. However, other research regulations may apply.

If the information is still identifiable in the research database, however, the Privacy Rule requirements for authorization or waiver of authorization should be applied to each new research project. In addition, the HIPAA Security Rule applies to how the database is maintained.

References

Department of Health and Human Services. 45 CFR §§ 164.512(i), 164.514; 42 CFR § 2.52, 2.62. Subpart A of Title 45 CFR Part 46; Food and Drug Administration. Title 21 CFR Parts 50 and 56. Documents on research databases and HIPAA available online from http://privacyruleandresearch.nih.gov/research_repositories.asp

Scenario 122

Is it okay to give the American Red Cross protected health information about a family member of a person in the military?

Alcohol and substance abuse laws

Because Federal Drug and Alcohol Treatment Programs do not deal with acute illness, this question is not addressed. Therefore, the patient must sign an authorization prior to disclosure of information identifying the patient as receiving these treatment services.

The HIPAA Privacy Rule allows the covered entity to communicate with the American Red Cross, the agency that provides emergency communications services with the military. The Red Cross is involved in notifying members of the military about members of their families who are ill or dead. The Red Cross also can assist the service person with obtaining emergency leave. In order to do so, Red Cross requires such information as: patient's name, nature of emergency (condition and/or life expectancy), name and location of the hospital, phone number of the hospital, and physician's contact information.

The covered entity should seek verbal consent from a patient before this disclosure, or may assume implied confirmation from the patient based on the circumstances. If the patient is unconscious or not able to consent, the healthcare provider can make the decision based on professional judgment as to what is in the patient's best interest. Therefore, when these conditions are met, there is not a requirement for an authorization for this disclosure.

References

Department of Health and Human Services. 45 CFR §164.510(b)(3). Department of Health and Human Services, Office for Civil Rights. Your Frequently Asked Questions On Privacy. 491. Available online from http://www.dhhs.gov/ocr/hipaa/.

Scenario 123

Are we required to give information to the military on active duty personnel?

 State and federal laws

Key words to search: consent, authorization, and mental or behavioral health treatment

 Alcohol and substance abuse laws

Federal Drug and Alcohol Treatment Programs require that the patient sign an authorization or a properly constituted order of a court prior to disclosure of information identifying the patient as receiving these treatment services.

There are specific standards in the HIPAA Privacy Rule that apply only to covered entities that are part of the Department of Defense or Department or Transportation. These covered entities are permitted to disclose information only to the Department of Veterans' Affairs when the individual is discharged from military service and only for the purpose of determining whether the individual is eligible for benefits. A covered entity that is also a part of the Department of Veterans' Affairs may disclose information about a veteran for the same determination of eligibility for Veterans' benefits.

There is also another provision in the Privacy Rule that permits any covered entity to disclosure protected health information of individuals who are in the military to appropriate military command authorities. The Privacy Rule states that the Department of Defense (DoD) must publish a notice in the Federal Register that lists the names of command authorities who may receive the protected health information and the situations in which the protected health information may be provided.

This notice was published in 2003. It states that military command authorities are all commanders with authority over individuals in the military. The purposes for the disclosure are to determine compliance with standards and activities under the authority of DoD directives about physical fitness, disability evaluation, and assessments of nuclear weapons personnel. Information may also be disclosed to determine fitness for a particular mission. The DoD may also request protected health information to monitor the health status of the military as a whole. Finally, the DoD may need such information for casualty reports. The command authority requesting the information should provide a copy of the Federal Register and appropriate DoD directives or instructions in order for the covered entity to determine whether this disclosure is to be made under this provision of the Privacy Rule.

A military tribunal has authority to subpoena the protected health information of a person in the military.

If none of these exceptions apply, the covered entity should require an authorization before disclosing the records.

References

Department of Health and Human Services. 45 CFR §164.512(k).

Department of Defense. 2003. DOD Health Information Privacy Program. *Federal Register* 68(68):17357–8.

Scenario 124

What can we tell the media when they call? Is there such a thing as "cases of public record"?

Alcohol and substance abuse laws

Federal Drug and Alcohol Treatment Programs require that the patient sign an authorization or a properly constituted order of a court prior to disclosure of information identifying the patient as receiving Program treatment services.

The concept of "public record" usually applies to other types of records governed by state or federal public access laws, such as ambulance or police documents. Prior to implementation of the Privacy Rule, it was a common belief that the public had a right to know what was going on with well-known individuals. However, the HIPAA Privacy Rule protects the privacy all individuals, well known or not.

If an individual chooses to be listed in a facility directory, any caller who knows the patient's name, including news media, can be provided the patient's "condition described in general terms that do not communicate specific medical information about the individual . . ."

When high profile or well-known individuals are admitted to facilities, and they choose to be listed in the facility directory, common practice is to route questions about them through a person trained to deal with the media, such as a public relations person. Although it is also permitted by the HIPAA Privacy Rule to disclose the individual's room number or room extension to callers, common practice is to consult the individual before allowing such media calls or interviews.

When high profile individuals are unable to decide a facility directory preference, or for individuals who are victims of crimes or who are in police custody, it is recommended that the covered entity not list the individual's information in the facility directory for reasons associated with the individual's safety and privacy. In that case, any family members attempting to locate the individual should be carefully screened prior to being given information. Once family is available or the high profile individual recovers consciousness, he or she should be given the opportunity to agree to or decline being listed in the facility directory.

When individuals wish more information than their general condition to be given to the media, they may sign an authorization for the covered entity to disclose further information.

Of course, an individual or his or her family is free to disclose anything they wish, as they are not covered entities. Some individuals who are aware that there is a high level of public interest in their case, actually set up a public-accessible Web site in order to keep the public informed.

References

Department of Health and Human Services. 45 CFR §164.510.

Scenario 125

What procedure do we need to follow when we want to publish patient stories or pictures in an internal newsletter?

Alcohol and substance abuse laws

Federal Drug and Alcohol Treatment Programs require the patient to sign an authorization or a properly constituted order of a court prior to disclosure of information identifying the patient as receiving Program treatment services.

The HIPAA Privacy Rule does not appear to address the use or disclosure of patient-identifiable information in internal publications, except to the extent it may be considered customer service, or a general administrative activity under healthcare operations. Stories authored by individuals or as reported by a covered entity about the services provided by the covered entity, or even general information about an individual residing in a facility, are commonly included in these types of publications.

One issue that should be addressed is that many internal publications do not remain internal, especially if they are posted in more public areas in a facility or distributed by email. Or, the facility may decide that a particular article or story could be used to communicate to the public about its services in a more general newsletter or even an annual report.

To cover the possibility of external disclosures, it a good practice to have legal counsel design a consent document for individuals to sign in order to publish stories created by or about the individuals. Consents may also need to be signed by individuals prior to being photographed, in order to meet JCAHO and other legal requirements. When external photographers or videographers are used, a business associate agreement with these individuals may be in order.

Finally, an authorization should be obtained from the individual at the same time to allow the disclosure of the stories and photographs to "the public" as a class of persons, for the purpose of publications created for communication, marketing, or fundraising.

References

Department of Health and Human Services. 45 CFR §§164.501, 164.504, 164.508.

Scenario 126

Do we need a separate authorization to release psychotherapy notes?

 State and federal laws

KEY WORDS TO SEARCH: consent, authorization

Because of the sensitivity of the content of psychotherapy notes, the HIPAA Privacy Rule extends special protections to these types of documents. It is the only type of documentation that the Privacy Rule treats with special protections. It is also the only type of record for which the Privacy Rule requires an authorization be obtained before the psychotherapist can disclose information to other treatment providers. Psychotherapy notes refers to notes recorded (in any medium) by a healthcare provider, who is a mental health professional, documenting or analyzing the contents of conversation during a private counseling session or a group, joint, or family counseling session, and that are separated from the rest of the individual's medical record. Psychotherapy notes exclude medication prescription and monitoring, counseling session start and stop times, the modalities and frequencies of treatment furnished, results of clinical tests, and any summary of the following items: diagnosis, functional status, the treatment plan, symptoms, prognosis, and progress to date.

To underscore the sensitivity of these documents, the Privacy Rule makes an exception to the use of a compound authorization to disclose protected health information. If an individual wants other types of records to be disclosed, such as behavior health treatment records, in addition to psychotherapy notes, the individual must sign two different authorizations, one for the behavioral health treatment records and one for the disclosure of the psychotherapy notes.

If the individual wants psychotherapy notes disclosed to multiple locations, he or she is permitted to use a single authorization for this purpose.

However, a disclosure by authorization is permitted, not required, by the Privacy Rule. If the covered entity feels these notes should not be disclosed because it is not in the best interest of the individual or other persons mentioned in the notes, it can refuse to provide the information.

The individual can also be denied access to psychotherapy notes.

References

Department of Health and Human Services. 45 CFR § 164.501, 164.508(a), (b) (3)(ii), 164.524.

Scenario 127

How can we determine whether a government agency is acting as a health oversight agency or a law enforcement agency?

 State and federal laws

KEY WORDS TO SEARCH: healthcare provider and facility licensure, insurance commission, oversight of healthcare, investigative demand, subpoena, request for records, fraud, investigation, warrant

 Alcohol and substance abuse laws
In general, in order to investigate or prosecute a Program or an employee of a program, Federal Drug and Alcohol Treatment Program regulations require a court order authorizing the investigation.

Health oversight activities, as defined in the HIPAA Privacy Rule, are activities conducted by, or delegated by, federal, state or other governmental agencies. Health oversight authority is derived from laws or regulations and is always related to oversight of a healthcare system, healthcare providers, or government programs in which health information is necessary to determine eligibility or compliance. It is also considered health oversight when one of these agencies needs to enforce civil rights laws in which health information is relevant. Health oversight activities might include audits, investigations, inspections, licensure or disciplinary actions, or even criminal, administrative, or civil actions against those within the scope of their authority. Oversight includes that of healthcare plans, health benefit plans, healthcare providers, and healthcare delivery, as well as resolution of consumer complaints related to healthcare, review of pharmaceuticals, medical products and devices, and dietary supplements. It can include a health oversight agency's analysis of trends in healthcare costs, quality, and delivery, access to care, and health insurance coverage for health oversight purposes.

It is important to distinguish between these activities and other types of law enforcement activities. A covered entity is able to provide protected health information to a health oversight agency when an agency provides documents establishing its identity and authority. The evidence that a health oversight agency needs to provide to demonstrate its authority is usually defined by the law or regulation from which it obtains its authority. For example, a state provider licensing agency may need to provide an administrative subpoena, whereas a Medicare oversight agency may need to only provide a request for records. Also, if the health oversight agency has contracted with a private agency to perform health oversight, the private agency should provide evidence of that delegation of authority.

On the other hand, with law enforcement actions, usually authorizations, court orders, criminal investigation subpoenas, or other appropriate legal processes must be obtained. The covered entity must be provided evidence of these prior to the disclosure of protected health information.

The first step in distinguishing health oversight is to determine whether it is a health oversight agency that is requesting the information. These are common health oversight agencies: state insurance commissions, state health professional licensure agencies, Offices of Inspectors General of federal agencies, the Department of Justice, state Medicaid fraud control units, Defense Criminal Investigative Services, the Pension and Welfare Benefit Administration, the U.S. Department of Health and Human Services (HHS) Office for Civil Rights, the Food and Drug Administration, Social Security Administration and the Department of Education regarding beneficiary eligibility, Occupational Health and Safety Administration and the Environmental Protection Agency, the U.S. Department of Justice and the Equal Employment Opportunity Commission (EEOC) civil rights enforcement activities in regards to the Civil Rights of Institutionalized Persons Act, the Americans with Disabilities Act, or any data analysis activities performed by a public agency to detect healthcare fraud. Accrediting agencies, such as The Joint Commission, are not considered health oversight agencies.

The second step is to determine the focus of the activity. Usually, healthcare providers or members of a healthcare system are the focus of the health oversight agency's activity, not an individual. Rarely, an individual who is not a healthcare provider is a focus of a health oversight agency when that person may be trying to defraud a government healthcare program, for example.

Some government agencies have both health oversight and law enforcement authority. The Drug Enforcement Agency and the Federal Bureau of Investigation are examples of such agencies. When these agencies contact a covered entity, they usually will disclose the purpose of their request and provide the appropriate evidence of authority for the disclosure of protected health information.

References

Department of Health and Human Services. 45 CFR §164.501, 164.512(f)(1); 42 CFR § 2.66; Department of Health and Human Services. 2000. Final Rule: Standards for the Privacy of Individually Identifiable Health Information. *Federal Register* 65(250):82530.

Scenario 128

What special considerations apply to the disclosure of mammogram films and related information?

 State and federal laws, and the Federal Mammography Quality Standards Act

KEY WORDS TO SEARCH: inspections, biopsy, recordkeeping, communication of results to patients, medical records, mammography reports, consent, and authorization

There is a special federal regulation called the Mammography Quality Standards Act (MQSA) whose provisions govern mammography films and associated reports. This reguation supersedes any conflicting requirements included in the HIPAA Privacy Rule. However, there do not appear to be significant inconsistencies between the two regulations in regards to a patient's right to access and copy his or her own information. The regulation states that the patient can request mammogram films and reports, and the healthcare provider must answer the request within 30 days. This is consistent with the Privacy Rule requirements for patient access rights.

Although MSQA commentary recommends that a written authorization be obtained from the patient for transfer of films and reports to the patient or to another healthcare provider, the actual regulation only requires the healthcare provider to act "Upon the request by, or on behalf of, the patient . . ." The healthcare provider can therefore use a verbal request by the patient if the provider chooses to do so, rather than require a written one. The regulation does not define who can request mammograms "on behalf of" the patient.

Documentation retention requirements may exceed those of the Privacy Rule. A written authorization or log of the transfer of mammograms or results must be kept for 5 years, or 10 years if the patient has not had a sequence of mammograms performed by the healthcare provider.

Charges for copies are permitted, and should be related to the documented cost of copying according to MQSA. This is also consistent with the Privacy Rule's requirement for reasonable copying fees when an individual requests his or her own information.

Regarding other disclosures, the Privacy Rule allows covered entities to release patient information to an MQSA inspector without patient authorization, because MQSA inspectors are performing health oversight activities required by law. The Privacy Rule also allows a covered entity to release patient biopsy information to a mammography facility to assist them in meeting a MQSA medical outcomes audit, because the disclosure is to a person subject to Food and Drug Administration (FDA) jurisdiction, the disclosure concerns an FDA-regulated product or activity for which the mammography facility has responsibility; and finally, it relates to the quality, safety, or effectiveness of the product or activity.

A patient can complain about lack of access or unreasonable copy costs to the healthcare provider, or to FDA via the Facility Hotline at 1-800-838-7715; or by writing to the following address: MQSA Hotline, P.O. Box 6057, Columbia MD 21045-6057. Patients in certifying states should contact their state certifying agency directly.

References

Department of Health and Human Services. 45 CFR §164.512; HIPAA and release of information for MQSA purposes, available online from www.fda.gov/ CDRH/MAMMOGRAPHY/mqsa-rev.html#HIPAA; MSQA. 900.12(c)(2)(i), (ii); 900.12(c)(4)(ii), (iii), available online from www.fda.gov/CDRH/MAMMOGRAPHY/ robohelp/start.htm/.

Scenario 129

Are we allowed to disclose patient information to a poison control center?

 State and federal laws

KEY WORDS TO SEARCH: poison control, consent requirements related to treatment

 Alcohol and substance abuse laws

Federal Drug and Alcohol Treatment Program regulations do not permit a disclosure when it identifies the patient as part of the Program. The disclosure must either be made with a signed consent by the patient or without identifying the patient as being part of the Program.

Most states have poison control agencies established to assist in both the prevention and the treatment of poisoning. Even though they are not a covered entity under the HIPAA Privacy Rule, poison control agencies provide consulting services for treatment of individuals, and, therefore, disclosure of protected health information is permitted in the Privacy Rule for treatment purposes to these agencies.

Evidence of treatment involvement can be inferred when a healthcare provider initiates the contact in order to obtain recommendations for treatment. The treatment involvement may be less clear when another individual, such as a parent, initiates the call to the poison control center and is told to take the patient to a healthcare provider for emergency treatment. However, the poison control centers usually have sufficient information from the initial phone call to demonstrate their involvement in the case. To facilitate this process, a covered healthcare provider should create a protocol in cooperation with the poison control center on ways to verify the identity of persons calling on behalf of the poison control center when they call. The covered entity should educate its workforce about this situation so as not to impede appropriate care.

The other purpose of a poison control agency is one of public health: prevention or control of poisoning. In this role, the poison control center is often designated by the state as responsible for reporting certain information to either state or federal public health agencies.

If the poison control agency is designated as a public health authority for this purpose, a covered entity may disclose the requested protected health information as required or permitted by law for the purpose of controlling or preventing injury.

References

Department of Health and Human Services. 45 CFR §§ 164.502, 164.512(a), (b); 42 CFR § 2.12.

Scenario 130

Is it possible to allow parents access to a child's records on-line?

State and federal laws

KEY WORDS TO SEARCH: minor, parent, guardian, age of majority, consent to mental health treatment, custody of minor children

Alcohol and substance abuse laws
Federal Drug and Alcohol Treatment Program record regulations require that a minor sign an authorization to allow disclosure of records to a parent.

The HIPAA Privacy Rule defaults to state laws in regards to the access of personal representatives to minor's records. For a covered entity to provide access to parents to their children's protected health information, on-line or otherwise, is dependent on state laws. For example, if there is a state law that states a minor alone must authorize access to information for his or her mental health treatment, sexually transmitted diseases (STDs), or her pregnancy, this would prevent at least this type of information from being available to a parent in an on-line record.

Another item to check in state law is whether a parent loses parental rights to access a child's records upon loss of custody of the child.

Covered entities who have successfully implemented on-line access of parents to their children's records usually have a cut off age set for a minor's records to be available on-line. An age range of between 12 and 13 years has been recommended, in order to avoid issues of mental health treatment, STDs, or pregnancy. Most covered entities have not made attempts to be selective in what information passes; for example, to try to exclude a minor's STD-related information would be extremely difficult to implement. These covered entities also set expectations for parents about custody situations up-front: for example, the requirement that a parent establish evidence of custody or revocation of parental rights, as required by state law, in order to terminate access for the noncustodial parent.

The best systems also provide for an emergency revocation of access; for example, allowing a healthcare provider to request the access to the child's records by a parent to be terminated if the healthcare provider determines there is a risk to the safety of a child by the continued access.

References

Department of Health and Human Services. 45 CFR § 164.502(g) i–iii; 42 CFR § 2.14.

USEFUL LINKS

The following links, provided in the listed scenarios, are also included here as a resource. A list of other relevant links follows.

From Scenario 13: Department of Health and Human Services, 2000. 45 CFR §164.530(c)(2); Department of Health and Human Services, Office for Civil Rights. 2003. Incidental Disclosures. Available online from http://www.dhhs.gov/ocr/hipaa/guidelines/incidentalud.pdf; Department of Health and Human Services, Office for Civil Rights. Your Frequently Asked Questions On Privacy. Available online from http://www.dhhs.gov/ocr/hipaa/.

From Scenario 14: Department of Health and Human Services. 45 CFR §164.530(c)(2); Department of Health and Human Services, Office for Civil Rights. Your Frequently Asked Questions On Privacy. Available online from http://www.dhhs.gov/ocr/hipaa/.

From Scenario 15: Department of Health and Human Services. 45 CFR §164.530(c)(2); Department of Health and Human Services, Office for Civil Rights. 2003. Incidental Disclosures. Available online from http://www.dhhs.gov/ocr/hipaa/guidelines/incidentalud.pdf; Department of Health and Human Services, Office for Civil Rights. Your Frequently Asked Questions On Privacy. Available online from http://www.dhhs.gov/ocr/hipaa/; Department of Health and Human Services. 42 CFR § 2.2(a).

From Scenario 17: Department of Health and Human Services. 45 CFR §164.530(c)(2); Department of Health and Human Services. 42 CFR § 2.1; Department of Health and Human Services, Office for Civil Rights. 2003. Incidental Disclosures. Available online from http://www.dhhs.gov/ocr/hipaa/guidelines/incidentalud.pdf/.

From Scenario 18: Department of Health and Human Services. 45 CFR §164.530(c); Department of Health and Human Services, Office for Civil Rights. 2001. Minimum Necessary. No longer available in this version online from http://www.dhhs.gov/ocr/hipaa/guidelines/incidentalud.pdf.

From Scenario 23: Department of Health and Human Services. 45 CFR §164.530(c)(2); Department of Health and Human Services, Office for Civil Rights. 2003. Incidental Disclosures. Available online from http://www.dhhs.gov/ocr/hipaa/guidelines/incidentalud.pdf/. Department of Health and Human Services, Office for Civil Rights. Your Frequently Asked Questions On Privacy. 202. Available online from http://www.dhhs.gov/ocr/hipaa/.

From Scenario 34: Department of Health and Human Services. 45 CFR §164.512(e); Department of Health and Human Services. 42 CFR § 2.61(b); Department of Health and Human Services, Office for Civil Rights. Your Frequently Asked Questions On Privacy. 707,708. Available online from http://www.dhhs.gov/ocr/hipaa/.

From Scenario 42: Department of Health and Human Services. 45 CFR §164.512(f)(1); Department of Health and Human Services. 42 CFR § 2.61(b); *United States v. Morton Salt,* 338 U.S.632,651 (1950), quoted in Department of Justice, Office of Legal Policy, *Report to Congress on the Use of Administrative Subpoena Authorities by the Executive Branch Agencies and Entities 8.* (May 2002). Available at http://www.usdoj.gov/olp/intro.pdf/.

From Scenario 47: Department of Health and Human Services, 45 CFR §§160.103, 164.512(b), 164.508(b)(4)(iii); Department of Health and Human Services, Office for Civil Rights. Your Frequently Asked Questions On Privacy. 301. Available online from http://www.dhhs.gov/ocr/hipaa/.

From Scenario 54: Department of Health and Human Services. 45 CFR §164.510. HIPAA Updated Guidelines for Releasing Information on Conditions of Patients. American Hospital Association: 02/01/2003. Can be found online at www.aha. org/aha/advisory/2003/030201-media-adv.html/.

From Scenario 70: Department of Health and Human Services. 45 CFR § §160.103, 160.202, 42 CFR §§ 2.11, 2.12(b),(e). The Drug Addiction Treatment Act of 2000 (DATA 2000), Title XXXV, Section 3502 of the Children's Health Act of 2000; The Confidentiality Of Alcohol And Drug Abuse Patient Records Regulation and the HIPAA Privacy Rule: Implications For Alcohol and Substance Abuse Programs. Found online at http://www.hipaa.samhsa.gov/ Part2ComparisonClearedTOC.htm.

From Scenario 77: Department of Health and Human Services. 45 CFR §164.510(b). Department of Health and Human Services, Office for Civil Rights. Your Frequently Asked Questions On Privacy. 1067. Available online from http://www. dhhs.gov/ocr/hipaa/.

From Scenario 80: Department of Health and Human Services. 45 CFR §164.510(b)(3), 164.522(b), 164.520(b)(iii)(A); Department of Health and Human Services, Office for Civil Rights. Your Frequently Asked Questions On Privacy. 198. Available online from http://www.dhhs.gov/ocr/hipaa/.

From Scenario 81: Department of Health and Human Services. 45 CFR §164.510(b)(3), Department of Health and Human Services, Office for Civil Rights. Your Frequently Asked Questions On Privacy. 198, 488. Available online from http://www.dhhs.gov/ocr/hipaa/.

From Scenario 100: Glossary of Long-Term Care, which can be found at www.toddltc. com/NeedToKnow/Glossary.aspx#IndemnityPolicy/.

From Scenario 102: Department of Health and Human Services. 45 CFR §§ 164.501, 164.514(f), 42 CFR § 2.12(c)(4). Final Rule: Standards for the Privacy of Individually Identifiable Health Information. *Federal Register* 65(250): 82515 CR 1. Most Commonly Asked Questions and the Health Insurance Portability and Accountability Act of 1196 (HIPAA) also Known as the Privacy Rule. American Association of Healthcare Philanthropy, found online at www.ahp.org/government-relations/hipaa/faq-on-hipaa.php/.

From Scenario 103: Department of Health and Human Services. 45 CFR §§164.501, 164.506; Department of Health and Human Services, Office for Civil Rights. Your Frequently Asked Questions On Privacy. 710. Available online from http://www. dhhs.gov/ocr/hipaa/.

From Scenario 110: Department of Health and Human Services. 42 U.S. Code §
1230d-6(200); 45 CFR §§ 160.103, 160.402. Memorandum: Scope of Criminal
Enforcement Under 42 U.S.C. § 1320d-6. Azar, Alex M. and Coleman, Timothy
J. can be found online at www.worldprivacyforum.org/pdf/hipaa_
opinion_06_01_2005.pdf/.

From Scenario 111: Details about filing a complaint can be found on the web site for
the DHHS Office for Civil Rights at http://www.dhhs.gov/ocr/privacyhowtofile.
htm/.

From Scenario 122: Department of Health and Human Services. 45 CFR
§164.510(b)(3). Department of Health and Human Services, Office for Civil
Rights. Your Frequently Asked Questions On Privacy. 491. Available online from
http://www.dhhs.gov/ocr/hipaa/.

From Scenario 128: Department of Health and Human Services. 45 CFR §164.512;
HIPAA and release of information for MQSA purposes, available at www.fda.gov/
CDRH/MAMMOGRAPHY/mqsa-rev.html#HIPAA; MSQA. 900.12(c)(2)(i),(ii);
900.12(c)(4)(ii),(iii), available at www.fda.gov/CDRH/MAMMOGRAPHY/robo-
help/start.html/.

Department of Health and Human Services Office for Civil Rights http://www.dhhs.
gov/ocr/hipaa/.

Links to the regulation text, Frequently Asked Questions, Fact Sheets, analyses of
HIPAA and research, public health, alcohol and substance abuse, many other resources

All state pre-emption analyses

http://www.nacdsfoundation.org/wmspage.cfm?parm1=73#/. All state analysis, pharmacy sponsored. See disclaimers and policy. Last updated: State Laws Regarding
the Treatment of Minors: February 4, 2003; State HIPAA Privacy and Security
Regulations: December 31, 2005; State Data Breach Laws: December 31, 2005.
http://www.statehipaastudy.com/. 50 state analysis, by subscription, completed 4/2003.

State specific pre-emption analyses

http://www.bricker.com/legalservices/practice/hcare/hipaa/preemption.asp. Links to
Alaska, California, Florida, Georgia, Illinois, Iowa, Kentucky, Maine, Nebraska,
New Hampshire, New Jersey, New York, Oregon, Texas, Vermont, Virginia, Washington. Some for sale, some free of charge.
http://www.aha.org/aha/issues/HIPAA/map/. Links to contacts for preemption by state.
http://www.healthprivacy.org/. Links to summary of state statutes, check to see if
current.
http://attorneygeneral.utah.gov/hipaa.html. Utah only, current.

State law links

Alabama http://alisdb.legislature.state.al.us/acas/ACASLogin.asp/
Alaska http://www.legis.state.ak.us/
Arizona http://www.azleg.state.az.us/
California http://www.leginfo.ca.gov/calaw.htm/

Colorado http://crs.aescon.com/
Connecticut http://www.cga.ct.gov/asp/menu/Statutes.asp/
Delaware http://www.delcode.state.de.us/
District of Columbia http://government.westgroup.com/
Florida http://www.leg.state.fl.us/statutes/
Georgia http://www.legis.ga/
Hawaii http://www.capitol.hawaii.gov/
Idaho http://www.state.id.us/legislat/legislat.html/
Illinois http://www.ilga.gov/legislation/ilcs/ilcs.asp/
Indiana http://www.state.in.us/legislative/ic/code/
Iowa http://www.legis.state.ia.us/IACODE/
Kansas http://www.kslegislature.org/
Kentucky http://www.lrc.state.ky.us/krs/titles.htm/
Louisiana http://www.legis.state.la.us/
Maine http://janus.state.me.us/legis/statutes/
Maryland http://mlis.state.md.us/
Massachusetts http://www.state.ma.us/legis/laws/mgl/
Michigan http://michiganlegislature.org/
Minnesota http://www.leg.state.mn.us/leg/statutes.htm/
Mississippi http://www.ms.gov/frameset.jsp?URL=http%3A/
Missouri http://www.moga.state.mo.us/STATUTES/STATUTES.HTM/
Montana http://data.opi.state.mt.us/bills/mca_toc/index.htm/
Nebraska http://www.unicam.state.ne.us/web/public/home/
Nevada http://www.leg.state.nv.us/
New Hampshire http://gencourt.state.nh.us/rsa/html/indexes/default.html/
New Jersey http://lis.njleg.state.nj.us/cgi-bin/om_isapi.dll?clientID=25311536
     &depth=2&expandheadings=off&headingswithhits=on&infobase=statutes.
     nfo&softpage=TOC_Frame_Pg42/
New Mexico http://www.nmcpr.state.nm.us/nmac/
North Carolina http://www.ncga.state.nc.us/gascripts/Statutes/Statutes.asp/
North Dakota http://www.legis.nd.gov/information/statutes/cent-code.html/
Ohio http://onlinedocs.andersonpublishing.com/oh/lpExt.
     dll?f=templates&fn=main-h.htm&cp=Phttp:/
Oklahoma http://www.lsb.state.ok.us/tsrs/os_oc.htm/
Oregon http://www.leg.state.or.us/
Pennsylvania http://www.pacode.com/secure/browse.asp/
Rhode Island http://www.rilin.state.ri.us/Statutes/Statutes.html/
South Carolina http://www.scstatehouse.net/code/statmast.htm/
South Dakota http://legis.state.sd.us/statutes/index.aspx/
Tennessee http://198.187.128.12/tennessee/lpext.dll?f=templates&fn=fs-main.
     htm&2.0/
Texas http://tlo2.tlc.state.tx.us/statutes/statutes.html/
Utah http://www.le.state.ut.us/
Vermont http://www.leg.state.vt.us/statutes/statutes2.htm/
Virginia http://leg1.state.va.us/000/src.htm/
Washington http://www.leg.wa.gov/wsladm/rcw.htm/
West Virginia http://www.legis.state.wv.us/
Wisconsin http://www.legis.state.wi.us/rsb/stats.html/
Wyoming http://legisweb.state.wy.us/titles/statutes.htm/

INDEX